Praise for the Book

Kathy Lamsargis, a retired teacher, has always worn one of the most important titles one could ever wear. She has played and continues to play a special role in my life and countless others. After 24 years in education, her commitment to nurturing students and fostering a love for learning is unparalleled. She possesses a unique gift for making complex ideas accessible, always encouraging curiosity and a space to grow.

This rare talent coupled with her boundless creativity and passion for storytelling will touch the hearts and minds of those who inquisitively open *Marbles in a Fishbowl*, bringing to life worlds that spark transformation, warmth and wonder. A book all generations can cherish together as she so masterfully highlights youthful yet trajectory shifting memories with her grandparents. Her captivating stories not only entertain but also enlighten, weaving lessons that resonate deeply.

As an Author, Kathy's rare ability to ignite curiosity and instill a lifelong love of learning through her lived experiences not only educates but profoundly transforms through guidance and care. Words she so eloquently shares as once a student and child and now as an educator and grandmother.

I consider it my privilege to have experienced Kathy's sagacious insights, superlative teachings and nurturing spirit up close. Now that you will experience her light, I know the world we share will only be better.

Marke Freeman
Speaker, sports analyst, CEO, Max-OUT Foundation and author of *Champion's Creed*

I have known Kathy Lamsargis over twenty years. She is my friend, a teacher, an international volunteer, and fundraising chairwoman and board member of International Assist Medical Missions (IAMM). It was common for families in Haiti and Nicaragua to walk many miles and wait for hours to get medical care. Kathy captured the hearts of those we treated by sharing stories and songs from her childhood. She had a close relationship with her grandparents. Now I can add that Kathy is a published author. I know her book will touch the lives of those who read it, the same way she has touched the lives of so many around the world.

Sandra Hudgins-Brewer RN, MSN, FNP
Executive Director, International Assist Medical Missions (IAMM)

Steeped in a sense of place and time, these vivid, heart-centered stories offer readers a chance to step back into the past and wander the streets of memory. This beautiful book brings to life decades and people long gone and evokes countless echoes of growing up with my own grandparents. Share this treasure with your children and grandchildren, and open a world to them they have never known, or enjoy looking back at the times that may have faded in your mind, reawakening the stories of your own past. This book will captivate readers of all ages.

Diana Henderson
Author of *Archangel Book of Days*, *Gathering of Angels*, and *Grandfather Poplar*

Marbles in a Fishbowl

Marbles in a Fishbowl

Kathy Lamsargis

ISBN-13: 978-1-944662-89-9

Cover Art & Design and Illustrations by Leigh Harris

Dedication

For my mother, Dorothy J. Walch,
the loving link to my beloved
grandparents, Roy and Jane Bode,
who nurtured my life by filling it with
love, joy, and memories that I
share with my grandchildren.

In loving memory of
my brother, Joseph Louis Walch,
11/13/1963-8/2/2024.

Acknowledgments

First and foremost, I offer my deepest thanks to my friend Paige Reynolds, who was my writing coach and patiently listened to my stories. She helped develop the content and provided guidance from start to finish. *Marbles in a Fishbowl* would not exist as a book without her. I am so grateful our paths crossed.

I wish to thank my illustrator, Leigh Harris, for her artistic talent in creating the cover and sketches. Your hard work added another dimension to the story. Thank you for your friendship and for encouraging me to take a leap of faith.

I extend thanks also to Diana Henderson of CreativeType.biz and Realization Press. Her keen eye and excellent attention to mechanical editing made all the difference.

My publisher, Drew Becker of Realization Press, displayed patience in answering my many questions as a first-time author. His outstanding knowledge and experience in the publishing world gained my respect.

Heartfelt thanks go to my friend Marke Freeman, a remarkable athlete and author of the book *Champions' Creed*. Her words inspired me to follow my dream.

My husband, George, doubted that I would ever stop revising my story but never had doubts about the end product. Thank you, George.

Last but not least, I want to share a special acknowledgment of family members who also had wonderful experiences with my grandparents: Dorothy Lee Kleindienst, Steve Bode, Stan Bode (deceased), Karen Recker, Jane Sites, Ed Walch, Joe Walch, and Rosie Burkett.

Table of Contents

Prologue

Roy Bode

Mississippi River

Crawford County, Missouri, 1910

*"Twenty years from now you will be more
disappointed by the thing you didn't do
than the ones you did do, so throw off
the bowlines, sail away from the safe harbor.
Catch the trade winds in your sails.
Explore. Dream. Discover."*
—Mark Twain

On a warm day in June 1910, twelve-year-old Roy Bode whistled with excitement as he prepared to go fishing with Pops, his grandfather. Edgar, his younger brother, begged to tag along and crouched down in the middle of the canoe with his favorite book, *Tales of Huckleberry Finn*. Pops grunted, lifting the weight of the canoe in his arms, and walked it out from the riverbank. Throwing one leg then the other over the side, he took his seat on the stern plank. A thin sheen of brown river water ran down his oiled cotton pants and puddled around Edgar. He raised his book above his head and declared, "Grandpa! Don't get my book wet!"

Half-heartedly Pops mumbled, "When you come fishin' with us, expect to get wet. Won't harm you none."

He dipped his oar into the water on the port side while Roy set a steady pace paddling at the helm. Roy knew how to read the sky and weather, watch for bugs biting on the river's surface, and listen for sounds along the shoreline. From the time Roy was "knee high to a grasshopper," Pops taught him to be curious. The sun felt warm on his face, and he thought, "What will I discover today?"

Along the banks, tall grass and cardinal flowers bloomed amidst the bushes. The sun blazed upon the steady and gentle current. In the distance, birds chirped from treetops. Roy pointed ahead and suggested they fish near an overhang of tree branches. Pops steered them closer. Tiny bubbles swirled and gurgled around decaying tree trunks.

Pops grinned and said, "Good spot. This will do." He patted his vest pocket, then pulled out a rolled cigarette and a small matchbox. He struck the match on his vest zipper, and it released a pungent smell of sulfur. A swirl of gray smoke circled in the air.

"What's our bait today?" Roy replied, "I dug up some juicy night crawlers and made a batch of stink bait."

Edgar gagged and pinched his nose as Roy opened the cooler. Roy chuckled, set the hook, and smoothly cast his bamboo pole. Within minutes, he felt a nibble, gave the line a short tug, and waited for the fish to take a bigger bite. When it did, he pulled the pole up and back. Pops taught him the routine. Reel it in a little, then let the line out, and repeat to wear the fish down.

He shouted, "I got one! Betcha he's a monster catfish!"

In a state of excitement, Edgar stood up and shouted, "Where's the net?"

The canoe dipped to one side and Pops growled, "Sit down, Edgar, or we'll all end up in the river!"

Edgar snapped back, "I didn't cause that. We hit something!"

Roy squinted. The glare of the sun made it difficult to see below the river's murky surface. Unexpectedly, a cluster of thick clouds hovered above, and Roy was horrified by what he saw. Edgar screamed and birds squawked loudly as they flew away. A garfish had snagged the bait and writhed helplessly between the jagged teeth of an alligator. His black beady eyes stared at them. He stretched over seven feet long and spiky knobs covered his leathery skin. When the gator wickedly slapped his tail, the canoe rocked.

Roy shouted, "What should I do? Let go of my pole?"

Pops yelled, "No! Pull him closer!" Without hesitation, Roy wedged his knees under the bow plank to gain leverage, gave it all he had, and pulled hard. The alligator started to roll and exposed its wide, smooth underbelly. Pops grabbed the line and swiftly cut it with his folding knife. The alligator dove below the river's surface, swam toward the shore, and disappeared into the tall grass. Pops sat down and breathed a sigh of relief. Edgar was hiccupping, something he did when he was nervous or scared. Roy gazed out over the mighty Mississippi. He felt exhilarated because he loved adventures like this.

The sun emerged and Pops chuckled. "We best be on our way before Roy's gator returns for dessert."

Edgar smiled and his hiccupping stopped. Roy glanced over his shoulder toward the shore. The river was quiet and calm. He felt an unfamiliar sense of invigoration and realized how grateful he was to be alive. Roy vowed to himself, "I'll never forget this day."

Jane Licklider

Oak Grove School

Crawford County, Missouri, 1910

"With courage you will dare to take risks,
have the strength to be compassionate,
and the wisdom to be humble.
Courage is the foundation of integrity."
—Mark Twain

It was graduation day in June 1910. Oak Grove was a one-room schoolhouse that stood on a small hill in Crawford County, Missouri, with a view of surrounding farms and the Mississippi River. On the last day before summer break, parents and students gathered for the ceremony and the annual marble competition. For Jane Licklider, fifteen years old, this day marked a bittersweet end to her education. Starting at an early age, she read stories aloud to the younger students every day. She would miss them but not as much as marbles and her friend Shorty. He was born prematurely during a bitter winter storm. He and his mother almost died. When one of his legs stopped growing, his father fashioned a special shoe for him. Unfortunately, it had a thick heel and caused him to limp. As a result, others teased him. When Shorty asked Jane to teach him everything she knew about marbles, she agreed. They stayed after school, where she taught him the rules and her "tricks of the trade."

Shorty's mother, a frequent volunteer at the school, prepared the tables. She approached Jane, gave her a gentle hug, and whispered, "Thank you for caring about my son. I am forever grateful."

Jane smiled sweetly and said, "Everyone deserves to be treated with kindness."

Their conversation was interrupted when Mr. Fitzpatrick, the headmaster, clanged the school bell and hollered, "Gather around, everyone! I have an announcement!" He waited until he had everyone's attention before he continued. "Jane Licklider has accepted a household position with a prominent family in the big city of St. Louis! She will be boarding the train later today, so keep her in your prayers for a safe journey!"

The crowd shouted words of encouragement. Mr. Fitzpatrick, who was a fidgeter, unconsciously scratched at the big mole and whisker on his cheek before he hollered, "It's time for the Pledge of Allegiance. Boys, hold up the flags, straight and tall for all to see. That's right. Jane will get us started."

She placed her right hand over her heart. Her voice was clear and steady as she recited, "I pledge allegiance to my Flag and the Republic for which it stands, one nation, indivisible, with liberty and justice for all." Their collective voices echoed back over the river's surface like skipped rocks.

Shorty's father walked onto a raked patch of dry sandy soil nearby. He poked a stick in the ground and drew four lines to form a large square, the bystander boundary lines, then etched a big circle called the players' arena. In its center, he positioned thirteen target marbles three inches apart to form a cross.

Mr. Fitzpatrick gave him a grateful nod and shouted, "As a reminder, everyone must stand behind the straight lines to avoid interfering with the match." He pointed to one of the young Licklider boys and yelled, "Dayton! Stop running around and go stand by your father." He scratched his cheek again and pointed at the other parents to locate their children.

Mr. Fitzpatrick explained the school donated the target marbles, so it was a "game of keeps." He announced the competitors, Jane Licklider and Shorty Evans. This was Jane's last match. As a matter of record, Shorty was the youngest competitor ever. While the McIntosh brothers chanted, "Win, Jane, win," the Breuer brothers repeated, "Short-tee! Short-tee!"

Mr. Fitzpatrick raised his arms and declared, "Let the competition begin!" Jane untied her faded cloth bag and pulled out her favorite shooter marble, the Christensen agate. As she held it toward the sun, it radiated bright yellow streaks and pinkish orange flames. Shorty nervously removed his leather pouch from his overalls' pocket and selected a bright green agate, a secret gift from Jane.

Mr. Fitzpatrick flipped a shiny new Lincoln penny and cried, "Call it, Jane!" She awkwardly clamped her hands together in prayer.

"Heads!" she cried. He caught the coin and slowly opened his clenched fist. Shorty wobbled as he stood on his toes to peer into the headmaster's palm.

He exclaimed, "It's tails! I go first!"

Following tradition, Jane extended her hand, they shook, and wished each other good luck.

Outside the players' circle, Shorty leaned down on one knee and reflected on what Jane taught him. He "knuckled down," confidently flicked his finger, and swiftly knocked a cat's eye marble out of the ring. The crowd clapped enthusiastically. His confidence grew with each turn. First the gray ghost rolled out and then a zebra. On his fourth attempt, his green shooter followed the target, and both rolled over the boundary line. Shorty knew the rules. He picked it up and placed it next to his other keepers. Unfortunately, his turn ended. Jane positioned herself and shouted, "Dead duck!" Her shooter knocked out a marble; then it rolled back with top spin just inside the boundary line. Next, she focused on the red bird followed by a milky white marble and then an orange flame. The game continued until they each had six keepers. One cloudy blue target remained.

Shorty tugged at his collar as sweat trickled down his pale skin. He drew in a long breath, closed his eyes, and recalled Jane's advice: "When the game draws closer to the end, stay calm and focus."

Shorty drummed his fingers on the ground, knuckled down, and nervously flicked his green shooter. Everyone watched it bounce off the blue marble. Shorty prayed for the shooter to stop, and the crowd gasped.

Loud cheers erupted, and everyone rushed into the circle. As Jane gave Shorty a quick hug, she slipped her beautiful agate into his pocket. Jane's sister Mandy crossed her arms and stood alone. She scuffed her boot heel in the dirt and ran to Buck, their horse. Jane cried, "Mandy, wait!"

Shorty's older brother pulled him up to sit on his shoulders. They victoriously pumped their arms and chanted, "Short-tee! Short-tee!" As he bounced up and down, he cupped his hands around his mouth and yelled, "Jane! Hey, Jane! I'm gonna miss you, but I'll never forget you!"

Jane stood next to Buck and her blue eyes twinkled. Her heart overflowed with joy. She shouted back, "Shorty! You won! Fair and square! You can do anything you put your heart and soul into!" A stream of tears flowed down her rosy cheeks. She glanced up at a feathery white cloud shaped like an angel. She securely tied her bag of marbles to the saddle horn and climbed up. Jane glanced back at the school one last time and whispered a prayer of gratitude. Shorty showed her that anything was possible. She was no longer afraid to move away. She and Mandy settled into the saddle.

She held the reins loosely, clucked her tongue, and gently steered Buck toward home. A new life awaited.

At the whistle-stop, Jane's train approached with a blast of steam. After it screeched to a halt, the attendant stepped onto the grated stairwell and greeted Jane with a reassuring smile. A breeze tugged at her white cotton dress as she gave her father a hug. She turned to the attendant, gripped his hand, and clutched her black tin suitcase. After she boarded the train bound for St. Louis, she took a seat, stoically gazed through the window, and waved goodbye to her father.

Chapter One
First Sleepover

Normandy, Missouri

May 1960

"A grandparent is a little bit parent,
a little bit teacher,
and a little bit best friend."
—Anonymous

My grandparents, Jane and Roy Bode, lived in a small, comfortable house in Normandy, Missouri. On a warm spring Saturday in May, my sister Karen and I squirmed in the back seat of the car and asked repeatedly, "Almost there, Mom?" I was six years old and was so excited about my first sleepover. When the car stopped in the driveway, Karen leapt out. I struggled to keep up with my older sister as I lugged my Barbie suitcase up the concrete steps. Grandma stood on the porch and greeted us with a big hug. She motioned that Grandpa was in the backyard and said he was listening to a Cardinals' baseball game on his radio.

Karen dashed inside and plopped down on the grey couch. Tiny dust particles scattered in the air. I eased into the cushions and peered into a glass fishbowl sitting on the side table. A dark green plant floated on the water's surface; its stringy white roots dangled below. Long vines curled down the table, nearly touching the floor. Layers of beautiful marbles laid in the bottom in variations of red, orange, yellow, green, royal blue, and purple. The morning sun streamed through the bowl and cast a faint rainbow on the wall. I noticed one odd marble. It was bright green and larger than the others.

Karen hopped up and startled me when she pressed her finger against the bowl. The wavy, watery-like prism on the wall disappeared. Karen shared, "I like the marble that's yellow and green. It looks like two tiny kites tangled up in the middle." Her breath fogged the glass. "Hey! Did you see 'em?"

Two goldfish darted through the roots. The larger one swam around the ceramic bridge. Little bubbles appeared from its mouth. The smaller one bobbed up and down, and its big black eyes stared at me. I smiled back.

From the kitchen Grandma cheerfully announced, "Girls, thought we'd bake a batch of cookies. Come join me. I have a surprise."

Karen ran to the counter where the ingredients were set out and asked, "What is it?"

Grandma handed her a blue checkered apron. Her name was embroidered in bright red thread. I expected mine to match because my mother often dressed us like we were twins. I was happy to see my apron was red, and my name was stitched in blue. I gave Grandma a thankful squeeze and slipped it on.

Grandma directed Karen to the cabinet where the recipe box was kept. She said, "Find the handwritten card labeled 'Pinwheel Cookies.' Want to practice your reading, Karen?"

She wrinkled her nose, and said, "I suppose so."

With Grandma's help, we followed the instructions step by step. Karen measured the flour and dumped it into the metal sifter. I squeezed its red handle back and forth, and small white puffs floated in the air. We took turns adding the ingredients, except for the two eggs.

Grandma said, "I'm going to show you girls how to properly crack an egg."

Karen eagerly reached for the open carton, grabbed one, and accidentally dropped it in the bowl. The yellow yolk oozed out from under the broken shell. Using her fingers, she tried to separate the shell fragments from the slimy egg white, but they kept moving around.

Grandma said reassuringly, "We can fix this with a little magic. Watch." She picked up the bigger half-shell, held it like a scoop, and dipped it into the thick egg white. Like a magnet, the broken shell flecks slid right in.

I blurted, "Grandma! You know all the tricks!"

The squeaky screen door startled us when it opened. Grandpa hollered, "What's going on in there? Sounds like fun!"

Karen replied, "Grandma is teaching us how to bake cookies, and she just showed us a magic trick."

Grandpa chuckled and winked at Grandma. "Girls, come outside and help me water my flowers. Maybe we'll find a white rabbit in the garden today."

Grandma smiled. With a nod, she granted permission. She called out to Karen, "Hang your apron by the door!" before it slammed shut.

I lingered for a moment, wrapped my arms around Grandma and told her, "You're the best." Grandma's blue eyes twinkled, and she told me to run along and have fun.

Chapter Two
Treasures in the Attic

July 1960

*"And we know that in all things
God works for the good of those who love him,
who have been called according to his purpose."*
—NIV Bible, Romans 8:28

We returned to Grandma and Grandpa's for another sleepover the weekend before July 4th. It was hot and humid, but Grandma was busy in her kitchen frying donuts. Karen and I ran to her side and watched. Using two forks, she carefully turned the donuts after the edges turned golden. She wore her blue flowered apron to protect her from the hot grease. She handed us brown paper bags; mine contained cinnamon and sugar, and Karen's had powdered sugar. Grandma instructed, "Shake a donut in your bag then let it cool before you take a bite." We devoured a couple and washed them down with milk.

When we heard heavy stomps coming from the mysterious door in the hall, I cautiously followed Karen to investigate. The round brass knob turned slowly, and a shadow formed below the sliver of light. Suddenly it opened, and Grandpa stepped out and said, "Jane, you know they're curious. How 'bout I take them up to the attic?"

Grandma responded, "I'll take them. Wait a moment, girls." A plume of dust and warm air escaped, and I smelled an odor similar to Uncle Frank's pipe and Grandma's musty basement. Grandma led the way up the steps. From the window above, the sun illuminated the dark stairwell. As we neared the top, we heard "Pop! Pop! Pop!" outside. Karen stood on her tiptoes, looked out the small dusty window, and remarked, "The boys next door are lighting fireworks."

Grandma replied, "Well, your grandpa and I won't have any of that around here. Be careful. Don't step on the pink insulation, or you'll fall through the ceiling and land on my living room couch!" She chuckled with a smile and let her words sink in. "For land's sake, we don't want any broken bones today!"

Grandma rested her hands on her hips and glanced around. I was astonished. I felt like I was transported back in time. A bundle of turkey feathers tied with twine brushed up against my arm and tickled me. I giggled and Grandma shared, "My mother, Alice, your great-grandma, raised turkeys on our farm."

Grandma gave us permission to explore and sat down in a wingback chair next to an old dressing table. I picked up a tarnished silver hairbrush and hand mirror. As I looked at myself, I made funny faces. That's when I noticed a picture behind me in the mirror's reflection. A painting of a woman playing a piano was propped against the wall. Her eyes were fixed on the sheet of music, and her fingers hovered over the keys. Her brown hair was tied in a loose bun at the nape of her neck. Her long red dress had white pleated sleeves. Grandma noted, "I don't know much about that, only that it's been passed down through my family for generations."

Next to it sat a black tin case with a worn handle. I thought about my Barbie suitcase. Karen asked, "Is that dented old thing yours?"

Grandma reflected, "Originally it belonged to my Papa who carried it to the 1904 St. Louis World's Fair. I could smell the sweet vanilla scent of waffle cones and ice cream, as he explained when they ran out of ice cream cups, the baker nearby offered to twist his thin warm waffles into a cone to hold the ice cream. And that's how waffle cones came to be. Someday I'll tell you more of his wonderful stories." Grandma added, "Kathy, maybe you'd like to have this case. When you grow up, you can go out into the world to create stories of your own."

Karen rummaged through some old boxes and discovered a baby's christening gown and two white leather shoes. She held them up and Grandma said, "Those belonged to my baby sister, Cora." She asked Karen to put them away.

I lifted the lid of a large box labeled "Jane's Wedding Dress." Inside was a beautiful gown wrapped in tissue paper. I ran my finger over the trail of pearl buttons on its sleeve. Grandma said, "My mother was a wonderful seamstress and spent hours on the details." I held it to my shoulders and secretly wanted to put it on. As if reading my mind, Grandma smiled and said, "Someday I'll make a special dress for your wedding day."

Karen picked up a round box, pried it open, and pulled out a black straw hat with a band of white silk flowers. Grandma chuckled and said, "That hat belonged to my mother. There's a photo of her wearing it as she and my father posed on the front steps. Can you look for it?"

Karen and I struggled to flip the latches on a large steamer trunk. Together we lifted the lid and grinned at the treasures inside. The top tray contained a box of heavy lead toy soldiers, some skeleton keys, a collection of masonic pins, and a small jewelry box. Below the tray was a stack of folded quilts, embroidered aprons, and hand-sewn tablecloths. Karen spotted something and proclaimed, "I found an old picture!" She turned it over and read aloud, "Ernest Wycoff. It's a photo of a man wearing a uniform."

Grandma's eyes widened. She got up, carefully navigated to the trunk, and sat down on a green leather stool. She put her hand over her mouth. Her muffled voice quivered, "Ernest Wycoff." She tenderly ran her finger across his face. Karen and I stared at each other.

Grandma took a deep breath. "Ernest and I grew up in Crawford County. My last year in school I developed a crush on him. I never told anyone, but I had a feeling I'd marry him someday. Before I moved to St. Louis, I boldly asked him to write, and he did.

He wrote about the local happenings in Crawford County and shared his life dreams. He traveled many times to St. Louis, and we spent our time sightseeing. I fell head over heels for him. When he told me he joined the Army, I was instantly frightened. Weeks later, he received his orders, and I met him at the train station. He asked me to marry him. I was so happy I cried tears of joy and said yes. Every night I prayed for Ernest and his safe return. I wrote him often, but as the war dragged on, his letters were few and far between." Grandma sighed and her eyes glistened.

I moved closer to Grandma and rested my head on her shoulder. She was quiet briefly before she continued, "One day, I received a special delivery package from Ernest's parents. My heart pounded in my chest, and I imagined the worst possible news. Inside was a worn photo of me and a handkerchief I'd given him." Grandma wiped away a tear as she asked me to look for an envelope. Grandma's fingers trembled as she opened it and removed a tattered, handwritten letter. Her voice quivered as she read:

Dear Jane,

Today, we received a typed telegram from the War Department in Washington, D.C. We were informed that Ernest and his comrades in the 35th Division fought courageously and died in battle in the forests of the Argonne. He was awarded the Purple Heart medal for his bravery. We wish we could be there to comfort you. God will see you through this sorrowful time. Be strong. Over time, happiness will find you again.

Grandma pressed the hankie against her cheek and said softly, "I was inconsolable, but my family and friends said God must have other plans for me. Two years later, I met Grandpa at a dance in Crawford County. Wasn't long 'til I was smitten. Grandpa was different. We shared a mutual love of nature and a curiosity about the Mississippi River. He took me on boat rides, and I fell in love with the river. While he fished, I read. He became my best friend and mended my broken heart."

Grandma sniffled, wrapped her hankie around Ernest's picture, and returned it to the trunk. She cleared her throat and said, "Let's get some fresh air. I'm ready for lunch. Aren't you?"

We put things back where we found them. I gave Grandma a hug and asked, "Are you sad?"

Her eyes sparkled as she whispered, "Oh no. Some memories are sad, but most are joyful. If I hadn't fallen in love with Grandpa, I wouldn't have your mom or you. Now I'm blessed with lots of grandchildren to love. God is great and always has a plan."

Chapter Three
Bubble Bath and Baby Powder

"We didn't realize we were making memories.
We just knew we were having fun."
—Winnie the Pooh

Grandma had a way of making ordinary tasks fun. Karen and I enjoyed bubble baths at her house. After she plugged the tub drain, she'd pour Avon Daisy Bubble Bath into the warm water. As bubbles formed, the sweet scent of flowers filled the room. First Karen carefully stepped in, and then Grandma helped me scooch down into the fragrant water. Karen and I playfully blew handfuls of suds at each other. As we splashed and dunked our heads, I wondered out loud, "Do mermaids live in oceans or rivers?"

She laughed. "You've stumped me. Ask Grandpa. He'll know. Now, show me your hands. When your fingers are wrinkled, it's time to get out." She pulled the plug by its chain and wrapped it around the faucet. She draped fluffy pink towels around us to keep us warm while the water gurgled down the drain.

Grandma said, "I have a treat for you. Close your eyes. No peeking!" Grandma removed something from the windowsill and said, "OK. Open them."

Karen reached out. "It's a doll! I love the yellow ruffled dress."

I liked the doll's pretty blue eyes just like Grandma's. She pointed and continued, "Look here, under her cap," and revealed four small holes. She turned the kewpie doll upside down, sprinkled a dash of baby powder into her palm, and gently rubbed it onto my arm.

After we dressed in our matching pajamas, Karen climbed onto Grandpa's four-poster bed. She clung to the spindled post and gently bounced up and down on the mattress. After I scrambled up, Karen said, "Let's pretend we're pirates at sea. I'll be the captain. You be the lookout." Captain Karen pointed at the window and exclaimed, "I see a ship in the distance!"

I dropped to my knees and curved my fingers, pretending to hold an imaginary telescope. I looked around the room and gleefully shouted, "I see … Grandpa!"

He had quietly entered the room and wore a black handkerchief tied around his head. He laughed and shouted, "Ahoy, mates! I'm gonna search this pirate ship for stolen treasures! If you give me trouble, I'll make you walk the plank!"

As if on cue, Grandma walked in and played along. She said, "Why, shiver me timbers! I'll rescue you from this buccaneer! Then it's time for a bedtime story."

Grandpa snickered, "Blimey! I've been foiled!"

Karen and I giggled and crawled under the light quilt Grandma had pulled out from the cedar chest. She tucked it under the mattress, turned on the night light, and sat on the edge of the bed to tell us a bedtime story.

She began, "A long, long time ago, your great-great grandpa and his sons cut down trees to build their homestead and furnishings."

I looked around and asked, "You mean he made the dresser and this bed?"

Grandma nodded. "He sure did. See those leaf patterns in the wood? He carved them." She told us the log cabins were drafty and cold, so they stuffed large cloth bags with dried cornhusks, horsehair, and chicken feathers to sleep on and explained that ropes were stretched across the wood frames to keep the bedding dry and off the floor. Her eyebrows shot up when she asked, "Can you imagine? Well, that's the reason we say, 'sleep tight.'"

Karen frowned and scratched her arm. "I'd hate to sleep on a mattress like that."

I chimed in, "Me too!"

Grandma knowingly shrugged and added, "I guess that's something we should be grateful for, our warm comfortable beds."

Grandma gave us a kiss on our cheeks and tenderly whispered, "Good night. Sleep tight. Don't let the bed bugs bite."

Karen leaned up on her elbow and mumbled, "Did you say bugs?"

Grandma grinned and reassured her, "It's just an old saying. Never mind. As you say your prayers, think about all the things you're thankful for. Tomorrow will be a new day with new adventures."

After Grandma left the room, I rolled onto my side, gazed through the thin curtain, and whispered, "Karen, I love you to the moon and back."

Karen sleepily replied, "Me too, Kath."

Chapter Four
Pancakes, Petunias, and
Unusual Umbrellas

"First my sister, forever my friend."
—Anonymous

A month later in August, we stayed over at Grandma and Grandpa's again. The hot summer sun streaked through the bedroom window and woke me. Karen wrestled with the sheet, stretched out her arms, and accidentally bumped me on the nose. She sprang out of bed and sprinted toward the wonderful aroma wafting from the kitchen. I gently rubbed my nose, slowly yawned, and grinned with anticipation. I slid down the edge of the high mattress and shuffled down the hall.

The kitchen table was covered by a starched white cloth with red embroidered teacups. A jelly jar, filled with freshly picked flowers, stood in the center. Small bowls of mixed blueberries and blackberries sat next to two place settings. Grandma tied her blue and white flowered apron in the back and cheerfully greeted us.

"Good morning, girls! Hungry for pancakes?" She mixed the batter, then dipped her finger into a glass of water. Pointing downward, tiny drops of water sizzled in the pan. Grandma winked at me and said, "The temperature is perfect." She formed pancakes with the batter, and air bubbles rose to the surface and popped. After the edges turned brown, she carefully flipped them. Karen placed a ceramic pitcher of warm maple syrup next to the small jar of elderberry jelly. Grandma said enthusiastically, "Time to serve up some piping hot pancakes. Get your plates."

While Karen gobbled down her pancakes, I traced my fingers around the stitched teacups and reflected, "Mom doesn't use a table cover at our house."

Grandma replied, "Well, times are different now. When I was your age growing up on a farm, we didn't have store-bought things, except the essentials. Sewing made my mother happy, and she hummed while she stitched. She taught me how to sew and embroider, and I'm so glad she did. I enjoy it. My mother used to say, 'Anything worth doing is worth doing right.' I've never forgotten that."

Just as we were finishing our pancakes, Grandpa stepped up to the screen door and hollered, "Get dressed, girls, and come help me in the garden."

Karen grinned and spouted, "I'm done! Race you, Kathy!" Her fork clanked against her sticky plate before she dashed off to the bedroom. She flung open the suitcase, pulled out a summer romper, and quickly tossed the matching one to me. Karen ran a comb through her blond hair, then helped me untangle my thick brown curls. I folded my lace-topped socks, buckled my shiny black shoes, and followed Karen outside.

Grandpa was in the flower garden, pulling weeds. His pants were grass-stained at the knees. He wore a faded Cardinals cap. I noticed beads of sweat glistening on his forehead and arms. When he stood up, he groaned and stretched his back. He asked Karen to turn on the water spigot next to the back door. As a small stream trickled from the hose, he explained, "Petunias have delicate petals, so hold the hose low to the ground and soak the soil."

Karen replied, "Sure, Grandpa," but within minutes she appeared bored. A mischievous look crossed her face when she placed her thumb over the copper ring and sprayed Grandpa!

He gasped and said, "Oh, that's cold!" and grabbed the hose out of her hand. He laughed and roared, "Aha! I'll show you!" We sprinted across the yard, narrowly escaping his attempts to sprinkle us with water.

When the back door slammed, we stopped in our tracks. Grandma burst into laughter and strode toward us. An old Brownie camera swung back and forth around her neck, and she carried two umbrellas. She urged, "Looks like I'm just in time! Don't want you girls to get sunburned!" She looked up at the clear blue sky and added, "Or rained on!"

Karen giggled and said, "It's not going to rain, Grandma!" as she snatched the black shiny umbrella. It had a bird head carved into the wood handle. The chrome bar slid up with ease and flapped open. I took hold of the other umbrella. It was made of bamboo, and the colorful pleated paper displayed pretty hand-painted flowers. As I awkwardly inched the center pole up and down, it crackled like a crunched bag of potato chips before it begrudgingly opened.

Grandma called us to the porch steps and said, "Girls, I want to snap a picture of you in your rompers holding the umbrellas. Your mom will love it!" Positioning the camera over one eye she instructed, "Say CHEEEZZ and give me a big smile!" We heard a *zzzsspp* sound as Grandma used her thumb to manually advance the film. "One more!" she shouted.

Karen stared at the handle on her umbrella and whispered into my ear, "Trade me." I hesitated, but to avoid a fuss, I obliged.

We gleefully skipped past Grandpa, twirling our umbrellas. We taunted him and begged him to squirt us. This time, he pelted us with water. We spun around in circles, wobbled from dizziness, and flopped onto the ground.

Karen screamed, "Oh no!" I crawled to her, hoping she wasn't hurt. Grandma calmly walked over to Karen and stood with her hands on her hips. Karen sobbed, "Look, Grandma! My clothes are ruined!" Her soaked paper umbrella had fallen apart. The blue, red, and yellow paint ran together, and a brownish color had splattered her shoes and socks.

Grandma sighed, pulled her up, and reassured, "Karen, you're fine. We'll get you cleaned up in a jiffy."

I watched them walk arm in arm toward the house and thought, "I'm so lucky to have a kind and patient Grandma." I dragged the broken umbrella to the back door and paused before going inside. I heard Grandma say, "You know, Karen, we can wash your socks and buy new shoes. Material things will come and go. But if you treasure your relationship with your sister, you'll have each other for the rest of your lives. Remember that."

Chapter Five
Warsh Day

"The first to apologize is the bravest.
The first to forgive is the strongest.
The first to forget is the happiest."
—Author Unknown

Every couple of weeks, Mom dropped us off at Grandma and Grandpa's for weekend visits. Summer weather skirted by. Karen and I returned to school in September. The leaves on the oak trees on my grandparents' street turned orange and red. An earthy, distinct fragrance of falling leaves filled the autumn air. One crisp October Saturday, Karen and I helped Grandpa rake leaves. We made big piles, jumped inside them to hide, and called for Grandpa. The metal prongs on his rake twanged against the hard ground as he neared. He laughed and shouted, "Karen! Kathy! Where are you?"

We screamed, "Here we are!" We jubilantly jumped up and tossed red and golden leaves at him.

Grandma shouted from the kitchen window, "Girls! I need a hand with the warsh."

Karen laughed as she tugged leaves from her hair. "Why does she say it that way? There's no R in wash."

I brushed off my clothes and said, "I bet that's what they called it on the farm. I kinda like it."

When we entered the house, the kitchen smelled like freshly cut lemons. I heard a repeating tick-tock on the wall and stared at the kit-kat clock marking the seconds with its tail. Karen looked around and yelled, "Grandma?"

A muffled reply came from the basement. "I'm down here!"

While we made our way down the steps, Karen pinched her nose, a sure sign she didn't like the musty odor. Grandma was singing a familiar tune, "You'll never know, dear, how much I love you…" She continued to hum the song's melody as she unlatched a small window, propping it open with a brick. Brittle leaves pressed against the screen, and their scent wafted in along with the fresh air.

Karen and I sang along, "Please don't take my sunshine away!"

Grandma reached into a box of dry soap, filled a small tin cup, and tossed the soap into the old Maytag washer. While the tub filled, she swished her hand to create suds. I stared at the gray wringers. They looked like two wrinkled rolling pins. Grandma fed a bed sheet into the rollers and cranked the long side handle. As the sheet poked out the other side, Karen carefully pulled it, and guided it into my outstretched arms, then into a large basket.

After we finished, Grandma warned, "Step back!" and pulled the plug. Gray water streamed out and swirled around the drain. As Grandma refilled the washer for the rinse cycle, Karen begged, "Can I have a turn? I want to feed the laundry into the rollers. Please."

Grandma took Karen's hand, palm up, and tickled it. She teased, "Do you want your fingers to get sucked in and crushed? What a bloody mess that would make!"

Karen yanked her hand. Grandma added, "I'll let you crank the side handle. OK?"

Karen replied, "I can do that." After the basket was full again, we helped Grandma carry it up the stairs.

A brisk wind tugged at my flannel shirt, but the sun felt warm on my face. Karen and I lugged the basket to the clothesline, which consisted of two metal T-poles and four lines of rope knotted at each end. A tattered cloth bag on a wire hanger held the wood clothespins and rocked back and forth with each windy gust. Karen hung a pillowcase by its corners, and I did the same with the next one. We took turns and created a long colorful banner of towels, shorts, and shirts. Grandma hung the bed sheets last. As they flapped in the wind, Karen cried out, "Kathy, look! Our pirate sails!"

I was tired and sat down on Grandpa's bench to watch the birds. A bright male cardinal perched on Grandpa's platform feeder. One by one, his orange beak cracked the black sunflower seeds. He ate the inner soft seed and spit the black shells to the ground. He whistled, "Cheer. Cheer. Cheer." followed by three chirps, "Birdy. Birdy. Birdy." A pale red female cardinal darted from a cedar tree branch and clung to a suet feeder. The wire cage was filled with Grandpa's special recipe of cracked corn, oats, and lard. A large blue jay startled me when it dove down to the ground feeder. The cardinals swooped back into their hidden nest. The jay bird's crown of blue-pointed feathers snapped to the left and then to the right. Like a thief, he promptly stole a peanut and fled to the top of the house.

In the vegetable garden, Karen plucked long string beans from their vines while Grandma pulled carrots out of the soil. Karen asked, "Can we carve the pumpkins this weekend?"

"I think it's a little early to carve them. They might rot before the end of the month," Grandma replied.

Karen looked disappointed. A pair of chattering squirrels chased each other around a nearby tree trunk, making it difficult for Kathy to hear Karen and Grandma's conversation. Suddenly, Karen stood up and shouted, "Kathy! Grandma's going to pay us for doing chores. We get to split all the loose change in her pocketbook for helping today!"

I shouted back, "Thanks, Grandma!" and bolted to the house. I rushed into the living room and jerked my polka-dot piggy bank off the shelf. My shoe slipped on the polished floor. I screamed as I tried to stop my fall but landed hard with a loud crash! The ceramic pig hit the wall and broke into big, jagged pieces.

Grandpa heard the commotion and ran inside. His voice trembled. "Are you hurt, Kathy?"

I whimpered, "I don't think so." Grandpa pulled a handkerchief out of his pocket and wiped my tears. He helped me get on my feet and guided me to the gray couch.

When Karen ran into the room, she immediately grabbed the other bank and pressed it against her chest. Grandpa bent down and carefully placed the sharp broken pieces into his palm. He tried to console me and said, "I think I can fix it. It's like a puzzle. Here's the letter K and the A. They fit together. See." Grandpa glared at the floor and mumbled, "Where's the T?" He turned over another piece with an R on it and sighed. He looked directly into Karen's eyes, searched for the right words, and said, "Sweetie, can you show me the front of your bank?"

Perplexed, she replied, "Why?" In the next moment, she understood. Her eyes swelled with tears and she cried, "No, Grandpa!"

I peered over the sofa and held my breath. Grandma quietly stepped forward from the doorway. Anticipating more tears or worse, she tenderly looked at Karen and gently pried the bank from her grip. The shiny red letters read KATHY. Karen plopped down on the floor and cried.

Grandma whispered, "Accidents happen. When they do, sisters don't hold grudges. They forgive. It's not easy but it's necessary."

I wiped my nose on my shirt, and Karen sniffled. I apologized. "I'm really sorry, Karen. I thought I had my bank. I'm sorry it was yours that broke."

She nodded and replied, "It's OK. I know you didn't mean it. Grandpa said he can fix it. I hope he can."

Chapter Six
Trip to the Stilt House

Elsberry, Missouri

May 1961

Travelers' Prayer
"May the road rise up to meet you.
May the wind be always at your back.
May the sun shine warm upon your face,
The rains fall soft upon your fields.
And until we meet again,
May God hold you in the palm of His hand."
—Anonymous

Before I was born, my grandparents built a stilt house on the Mississippi River. Karen and I heard many stories about it, and we couldn't wait for our first trip there. Just before Memorial Day weekend in 1961, Grandpa and Grandma prepared for their summer vacation at the stilt house. Grandpa washed and polished his black Ford Fairlane and checked the oil, the wiper fluid, and the tire pressure. He cleaned out the trunk to make room for Grandma's meticulously organized boxes of food and supplies. After Karen and I clamored into the backseat, Grandma gave us coloring books and a tin cigar box filled with crayons. As we pulled out of the driveway, I rolled down the window. The warm air blew against my face and helped me contain my excitement.

Grandpa drove onto the main road and declared, "Girls, we are in Lincoln County, heading north on Highway 79. Timberlake is over an hour drive, so settle in."

Karen wondered aloud if President Lincoln lived nearby. Grandpa pushed up his glasses and said, "No. Abe Lincoln grew up in Indiana. When he was a young man, he moved to Springfield, Illinois, where he became a lawyer. That was before he got into politics."

Grandma handed Karen a chilled bowl of green grapes and apologized to Grandpa for interrupting. Karen plopped two in her mouth, then passed the bowl to me. Grandma smiled and insisted, "Chew slowly. No choking allowed on our way to Timberlake."

Grandpa leaned forward against the steering wheel and announced, "See ahead! The sign reads 'Welcome to Old Monroe.'" He tapped the brakes, and the car gently bounced over the railroad tracks.

I asked if President Monroe lived here. Grandma looked over her shoulder and quizzically replied, "Did you learn about the presidents in school? As a matter of fact, President Monroe was from Virginia. He was our fifth president. Isn't that right, Roy?"

Grandpa grinned at her and nodded.

We stopped at Winfield to get gas and pulled into the Sinclair station. A bell rang and a young attendant approached the car. I pointed up and laughed, "Hey, there's a big green dinosaur on the sign."

Grandpa spoke to the attendant, jingled some coins in his pocket, and headed for the Coca-Cola machine. He bought four ten cent bottles. He said, "These two dimes are for your piggy banks. Save 'em for a rainy day."

We thanked him and sipped our sodas. While the attendant washed the windshield and pumped the gas, cars lined up at the Winfield Ferry crossing. A returning barge, guided by a small tugboat, docked on the beach.

Grandma explained, "That ferry provides a shortcut to the Sandy Island Bald Eagle Sanctuary. Maybe we'll visit there sometime."

Karen shouted, "Bald eagles? I've never seen one! Can we go now?"

Grandma shook her head and replied, "Maybe on our way home at the end of summer."

Several more miles down the road, Grandpa chuckled, "Don't blink or you'll miss the town of Foley."

I tapped Karen on the shoulder, giggled, and blinked my eyes.

For the remainder of the drive, Grandma embroidered and reminisced. She shared stories about her sister Mandy and her husband Frank and talked about how they helped build the stilt house and the fun they had that first summer. She added, "That's why we nicknamed it 'the clubhouse.'" Grandma stared out the window and remarked, "The weather was so nice that year. We decided to stay until Labor Day. While we were packing up, a real estate agent posted a Land for Sale sign next door. I told Mandy it must be divine intervention, and they bought the land that very day. We spent our second summer at Timberlake helping Mandy and Frank build a stilt house like ours. The rest is history, as they say." She smiled affectionately at us.

Grandpa broadcasted, "We're here, girls! See the sign? Welcome to Timberlake!" I stuck my head out the window and tried to get a good look at the stilt house. It was exactly like Grandma's pictures: a wood box on tall stilts facing the Mississippi River. As soon as the car stopped, Aunt Mandy and Uncle Frank rushed over while shielding their eyes from the dust. Uncle Frank hauled water jugs from Grandpa's Ford to the fish station, and Aunt Mandy grabbed a big box of supplies. Before she headed up the stairs, she removed mud from her shoes with the old-fashioned metal scraper bolted to the ground. When Karen dashed toward the river, Grandpa told her to stop and help unpack. I inhaled the sweet smell of cedar and glanced around.

Grandpa's fishing boat was tied to the dock and gently rocked in the river. Frothy white foam lapped against the bank. Karen and I carried our suitcases inside, but Grandma stopped us and told us to remove our shoes. The wood planks at the entrance were rough, but a paisley rug covered most of the room. It felt soft under my bare feet. Grandma instructed us to remove the furniture covers from the couch, chairs, and tables. Karen and I held the sheet corners and gently waved our arms to shake off the dust. They billowed like parachutes as we slowly stepped toward each other like we were waltzing. We folded and stored them in the front coat closet.

I noticed butterscotch candy in an acorn shaped dish on the side table. I asked, "Can Karen and I have some candy, Grandma?"

Bacon sizzled in a skillet and she replied, "I'd rather you wait until after we eat."

Karen shrugged and said, "OK. Anything else?"

Grandma replied, "No, thanks, girls. Go see what Grandpa is up to. I'll holler when the food is ready." Karen leaned into my ear and whispered, "Race you to the dock!"

After a light meal of BLT sandwiches, chips, and fresh strawberries, Aunt Mandy and Uncle Frank wandered over. We all sat on the porch and watched swirls of cotton candy colors spread over the river. Grandma sighed and said, "Girls, it's time to get ready for bed. Let's head to the kitchen for a bath."

Karen cocked her head and said, "What? A bath in the kitchen?"

I giggled, and Grandma grinned. She poured water into a kettle and placed it on the back burner. She struck a wood match on the counter's metal trim and ignited the pilot light. Purple and blue flames danced around the pot's bottom. Grandma said, "Safety first," slipped potholder mitts over her hands, and poured the warm water into the sink. After she added a splash of cool tap water, she checked the temperature with her elbow. "Just right," Grandma whispered. She parted the curtain below the sink and retrieved a bar of Ivory soap and two washcloths. Karen stepped up on the stool first. When she finished washing, it was my turn.

As the sun hovered above the horizon, we changed into our pajamas. Aunt Mandy and Uncle Frank retreated to their stilt house. Grandpa and Grandma played card games with us on a folding table until it was time for Grandpa to set up the cots. He positioned them near the windows and placed thin mattress pads on top. Grandma flapped a flat sheet for each cot before she tucked the corners into the springs. Karen and I were mesmerized by blinking fireflies near the river's edge. Thousands of stars twinkled above, casting shimmering reflections on the river's surface. I closed my eyes and listened to the bullfrogs and their low bellows. But a different sound perplexed me. It was rhythmic. Was it crickets or locusts? It sounded like marbles clicking against one another. Before I fell asleep, I thought, "I'll ask Grandma in the morning. She'll know."

Chapter Seven
Fishing on the Mississippi

*"Give a man a fish and you feed him for a day.
Teach him how to fish and you feed him for a
lifetime."*
—Lao Tzu

Time at the clubhouse was measured by the rise and fall of the sun on the river. One overcast morning in June, Grandpa woke us up. "Girls!" he shouted, "We're goin' fishin' today!"

As Grandma helped Karen into her lifejacket, Karen complained, "I don't want to wear this stinky thing."

Grandma scrunched her nose playfully and explained, "Well, you must. It's for your protection. If you fall in the river, it'll keep you afloat. You can't take chances with the powerful Mississippi currents." Grandma smiled and clicked the metal buckles into place.

Karen frowned and stared at the murky water below the dock. Grandpa handed me a shoebox full of soil and wiggling nightcrawlers.

Grandma gave Karen a brown paper bag and said, "I made sandwiches if you get hungry."

Grandpa gathered the poles, picked up the cooler, and the three of us headed to the dock.

Grandpa stepped inside the boat, balanced himself, and took our hands to guide us to our wooden seats. After we got situated, he firmly gripped the motor and pulled the cord. When it sputtered and died, he insisted, "Don't worry, girls! I'll get this old boat running."

He adjusted the throttle, pulled the cord again, and it began to chug. Bluish green puffs of smoke hung in the air. From the stilt house, Grandma waved both hands and shouted, "Go get 'em, girls! We'll have fried fish for supper!" Grandpa waved goodbye, made a wide smooth turn, and steered the boat through the channel.

Grandpa Roy grew up on a farm near the river. He used to say that his first love was the Mississippi River. He learned how to fish from Pops, his grandfather. Later in life, after he married Grandma, he joined the union and learned how to work the tintype presses. Grandpa was a handyman and liked to build things. He was also a big fan of baseball, specifically the St. Louis Cardinals. He spent hours in the backyard crafting fishing lures and listening to baseball. A Marlboro cigarette always dangled from the side of his mouth. I wanted him to quit smoking but was afraid to speak up. I wish I had. On fishing days, he wore his faded vest and lucky hat. Sparkling metal and feather lures dangled from both. I was curious about the string of white calcified stones that were strung like a necklace around the brim of his hat.

Grandpa steered us toward a small island. Karen rocked the boat when she stood up and pointed. "Do people live there?"

He told her to stay seated, dipped his cigarette into the water, then shoved it into a tin can filled with sand. He teased, "Local folks claim wild pigs roam there at night, and you can hear 'em squealing as they prey on helpless varmints!"

He chuckled and Karen shook her head. "Oh, Grandpa! I know you're kidding!"

He snorted like a pig to make us laugh. He slowed the motor to an idle, and the boat drifted toward a cluster of low-hanging branches. He grabbed them and pulled the boat closer. Grandpa tossed a small rusty anchor overboard and proclaimed, "This fishin' hole looks good." He dug his fingers into the shoebox and pulled out a fat worm. It squirmed relentlessly as he threaded it onto a sharp hook. Karen and I grimaced, grateful we did not have to do it.

Karen quickly tried to cast out, but her line got tangled in the branches. Frustrated, she yanked her pole loose and startled a flock of birds. They screeched loudly and flew off. Grandpa frowned, took her pole, and asked her to slow down. He grumbled something under his breath. I couldn't understand what he was saying. He looked at me and said calmly, "Kathy, while I put more bait on Karen's hook, I want you to follow my instructions. OK?" I nodded and listened. He continued, "Hold the line with your thumb and cast from the side; a short distance will do. Release the line and keep it loose until you feel the bait land on the river's bottom. Wait a second or two, and then give it a gentle tug. That's how we tease the fish to bite. Understand?"

I said, "I think so," and awkwardly cast out. A tiny circle formed around my line as it disappeared below the river's surface. I was proud. Now and then, I gave the line a gentle tug. Minutes stretched into an hour, and I didn't see or feel the line move. Neither did Karen. When she yawned, Grandpa cleared his throat and said, "Well, it seems the fish are eating their lunch somewhere else. Reel in your lines, and let's see what Grandma packed."

Karen opened the brown paper bag and pulled out a sandwich wrapped in wax paper and bound by a rubber band. When Grandpa opened it and took a big bite out of his liverwurst sandwich, Karen pinched her nose and cried, "Oh! That smells awful! What is that?"

Grandpa smiled and replied, "My favorite!"

Karen hesitantly unwrapped the other two sandwiches and handed one to me. I held my breath, then realized what it was. I grinned and excitedly remarked, "It's our favorite: peanut butter and jelly with no crust!"

Grandpa grinned, brushed crumbs off his hands, and asked, "What we got for drinks?"

Karen opened the cooler and passed a chilled can of Coca-Cola to me. With that mischievous look she gets before she pranks Grandpa, Karen exclaimed, "Oh no! There's only one more Coke!"

Grandpa hollered, "What? I don't get one?"

She rummaged through the ice cubes, whisked out a can, and burst into laughter. "Here's your soda, Grandpa! I was just kidding."

He sat back and pulled the tab: *kachoo.* White foam spilled out of the opening like a volcano, and he slurped it up. After a few gulps, he emptied the can and burped loudly.

Karen scolded, "Grandpa!"

He didn't say anything. I couldn't help myself and giggled.

He finally responded, "You know, my grandpa taught me how to fish. Now it's my turn to teach you and Kathy." He asked Karen to find the bar of Ivory soap in the tackle box. He unwrapped the soap and started carving small chunks.

He began, "I remember the first time Pops took me fishing. The weather was mild and overcast like today with a hint of rain in the air. Late in the afternoon, we pushed off from shore. We had to row in those days. When we got to the fishin' spot, he patiently taught me how to thread the worm. I didn't mind. After I cast out, I got bites right away, but they stole the bait and swam off. After a while, I got tired. It was around twilight, and I curled up in a ball on the canoe's bottom. Strange drum-like sounds lulled me to sleep. When I woke up, the sky was filled with a milky glow and millions of stars. Pops called it the Milky Way. In the distance down the channel, I noticed some flashin' lights. They got bigger as they got closer. It was a steamboat, and strings of lights bounced on the deck. The passengers wore fancy clothes and musicians played ragtime music. I was amazed, but Pops was furious. Waves pounded against our canoe. He cursed and called them good for nothin' paddle-wheelers. They steamed by and left us rocking in their wake. Pops pulled up the anchor and rowed down the channel. In the starlight, I saw tiny bubbles bumping against a rotting tree trunk. Pops sliced a piece of the lard soap, shoved it on my hook, and gave it a spin. I cast out and got a bite right away. I reeled in a drum fish and Pops told me about the lucky stones hidden inside. I was so excited and must've caught a dozen drums that night. Ever since, I've been angling for drum fish."

Grandpa removed his hat and ran his fingers over the stone necklace. He glanced upward and growled, "Shoot. By the look of the sky and clouds, rain is headin' our way. We'd better go home."

Karen sheepishly said, "I want to try your secret bait. Please, Grandpa. How can we go back without any fish?"

Grandpa sternly replied, "No. It's gonna rain. I'm certain."

Karen pouted, but I knew Grandpa was right. Dark clouds gathered, and by the time we reached the dock, it started to rain. Karen jumped onto the deck, but I raised my arms for Grandpa to lift me out. Karen ran ahead, threw her jacket and pole under the stairwell, and rushed up the stairs. I wasn't far behind. Grandma was at the stove, stirring a steamy pot of chicken and dumplings. My mouth watered. Grandpa stormed inside, shook his vest and hat, then hung them at the door.

Over her shoulder Grandma said, "No luck, Roy? Better luck next time. Girls, go wash up. Did you like your sandwiches?"

I gave Grandma a squeeze around her waist and whispered, "You betcha. Thanks, Grandma."

Chapter Eight
Baby Cora

*"Angels descending, bring from above,
echoes of mercy, whispers of love."*
—Fanny J. Crosby

After sunset, moisture hung in the air. The sky was black, and the stars were shrouded by ominous clouds. Twig like bolts of lightning cracked above the trees. Rolling thunder shook the clubhouse windows, and when the lights flickered Grandpa lit two kerosene lamps. I felt alarmed. Karen suggested we count the seconds between each strike. Grandpa taught us that. As the storm drew closer, Grandpa reinforced the window coverings facing the Mississippi. "Girls!" he barked. "You'll be sleepin' in the spare room tonight." He gave us flashlights and told us to keep them under our pillows. When the power went out, Karen and I shrieked. Grandpa held the lantern up to his face, grinned, and said, "Don't you fret. It's gonna be OK. Right, Jane? I'll be on the porch. Don't want to miss the show!"

The lantern swung in Grandma's hand as she led us to the spare room. I clung to her apron and followed her so closely I accidentally stepped on her heels. Karen and I scrambled onto the bed and burrowed under the covers. The lights continued to flicker, casting eerie shadows on the walls. Karen shined her flashlight around the room, screamed, and threw the blanket over her head.

Grandma shouted, "Good grief, Karen! What is it?"

I flashed my light toward the ceiling and muttered, "Who is that scary man with the m-m-m-mole on his face?"

Grandma chuckled. "Why that's nothin' but a silly old cutout. My friend Shorty made it for me. It's a funny reminder of our school headmaster, Mr. Fitzpatrick." Grandma went to the cedar chest, pulled out a light patchwork quilt, and spread it over us.

She sat on the bed's edge and told us a bedtime story about her family. Grandma began, "I grew up on a farm in Redbird. When I was your age, I helped Mama look after my baby sister, Cora. I loved her like she was my own."

Karen interrupted, "In the attic, the christening gown and shoes belonged to her. Right?"

Grandma nodded. "On a cold winter day, a storm blew in. Snow drifted around the door and windows. Poor little Cora's cheeks blazed bright red. Mama and I took turns placing a cold rag on her forehead, but she didn't stop crying. Papa hitched up the horse and wagon and promised to return with the town doctor. We didn't know then but learned later that a flu pandemic was spreading across the nation. My heart ached for Cora. I laid on the floor between the fireplace and her cradle and rocked her while I hummed. Mama was exhausted and fell asleep in her chair. After I placed a log on the fire, I prayed long and hard for Papa's safe return. I tried to stay awake but gradually fell into a deep sleep."

Grandma paused when Karen rolled onto her side. I propped myself up to listen. Grandma smiled and continued, "I dreamt about a glittery rainbow above the stars and moon, and it sang in harmonic tones. A little angel dressed in a christening gown and white booties floated among puffy silver clouds. Her face was hidden by ringlets of golden curls. She hovered in the sky like a hummingbird and softly called my name. She sweetly whispered, 'I love you' before her wispy wings fluttered, and she flew through a pair of golden gates into heaven."

"I woke up to the sound of Papa's voice comforting Mama, who was crying. His clothes were soaked, and he trembled. He told us that a large tree blocked the road, making it impossible to pass. He was forced to come home without the doctor. Mama wrapped her arms around me. She whispered, 'Cora died during the night and went to heaven where she's in God's loving hands.' I sobbed and hugged my parents tightly."

In loving memory ...

Cora Marie Licklider
Born 2-11-1912
Died 3-11-1913
Buried at Licklider Cemetery
Crawford County, Missouri

Chapter Nine
Circle of Stings

"Be a friend.
Encourage someone.
Take time to care.
Let your words heal and not wound."
—Author Unknown

August at the clubhouse was hot, and the mosquitoes relentlessly tried to bite my skin. Grandma said they liked me because I was sweet. As always, she had the best cure. She crushed pineapple weed flowers and leaves in a bowl to release a fragrant oil. Karen and I rubbed the mixture on our arms and legs to repel bugs, and it worked. The heat and humidity made me sluggish, so Karen and I listened to music on Grandpa's radio while we played jacks on the porch. Neither of us wanted to learn how to clean the drum fish we had caught, but Grandpa insisted. He stopped at the back door, hollered, "Let's get to it girls," and headed for his fish station. He built it with household scraps of wood. An old door served as the main tabletop, and it was propped up by wooden legs.

Uncle Frank trudged up his dock and across the lawn with a string of fish. Fumbling with his pipe, he mumbled, "Caught these catfish on my trot line. If you wanna skin 'em, Roy, you can have 'em." Karen and I stood behind Grandpa and watched him like we did Grandma when she cooked at the stove.

He unrolled a leather bag and displayed a dozen knives of diverse sizes and shapes. He selected one with an ivory handle and said, "Turn away, girls, if this makes you squeamish."

Karen covered her eyes, but I was curious. He made the first cut at the drum's head, sliced down the backbone, and located the thin white pin bones. He cut off that section and tossed the bloody parts onto a newspaper. He chuckled, "That wasn't so bad, was it, Kathy?"

Uncle Frank sat down on a tree stump, packed his pipe with tobacco, and playfully said, "Couldn't have done it better myself."

Grandpa winked at me before he said, "Time to find the hidden treasure." Karen perked up for a moment. He abruptly chopped off the head, threw it on the ground, and stomped it with his boot.

Karen howled, "Grandpa!" and gagged like she might throw up. Shocked by the sound of squishing muscles and breaking bones, I covered my ears.

Grandpa reached into the shattered skull and stated, "Here they are!" He pulled out two small ivory-colored rocks, dunked them in the water bucket, and dried them with his shirt. He rolled one between his fingers and said, "Look closely. Can you see the letter L?" I stepped closer and held out my hand. Grandpa explained, "The Osage native Indians that lived in Missouri before the settlers arrived carried them for luck. That's why they're called lucky stones. Keep 'em safe and you'll see." Grandpa glanced at the trot line and said, "Cleaning catfish is done differently." He gripped the head, sliced it down to the tail, and opened it like a book. He clamped a pair of pliers at the top and tugged the smooth skin downward. It peeled off in one piece.

As Grandpa tossed the catfish skin and guts on the newspaper, I noticed Aunt Mandy on the dock next door. Bits of straw fluttered around her as she vigorously swept spider webs off the rails. She stopped and screeched, "When are you going to fix this doggone rotten plank, Frank?"

He stretched his arms and groaned, "On my way, dear!"

Aunt Mandy complained, "Frank! I need your dang blasted help!" Her words ricocheted over the river, followed by a hair-raising wail.

Karen and I simultaneously shouted, "We're coming, Aunt Mandy!"

Karen arrived first. Her feet pounded the planks, making it hard for me to keep my balance on the swaying dock. Aunt Mandy was on her hands and knees, feeling for her glasses. Her hair was a mess. Loose strands escaped her bun and covered her face.

Karen implored, "I'll take one arm. You take the other. On the count of three. Ready, Aunt Mandy?"

She stood and wiped her nose with her apron then screamed again in agony. When Grandpa and Uncle

Frank trotted onto the dock, Grandpa's outstretched arm blocked Uncle Frank from moving forward.

Grandpa warned, "Everyone! Listen to me! Stand still!"

Karen asked, "Why? What's going on?" then gasped.

Aunt Mandy's eyes were bloodshot, and a circle of red spots swelled around her lips.

Grandpa repeated, "No sudden movements! Walk slowly toward us."

Uncle Frank took Aunt Mandy's hand to guide her up the ramp. Grandpa urgently instructed us to find Grandma, and bring the jar filled with honey and Borax.

I told Grandma what happened and pointed to Grandpa. Six feet away angry hornets buzzed aggressively around their nest. They zipped up and down, in and out like a boxer jabbing at his opponent. She rushed to Grandpa's side, opened the mason jar, and poured a sticky mixture into the lid. Grandpa cautiously stepped a foot closer to the swarm of hornets and prudently placed the deadly concoction on the rail. Grandma and Grandpa shuffled toward the clubhouse in silence. He said, "I'll bet Mandy thinks twice about yelling at Frank like that again."

I met them at the fish station and heard Grandma say, "Thanks to your quick thinking, no one else was stung." She smiled warmly, patted his shoulder, and reminded him, "Mandy is gonna be in a world of hurt for the next few days." Grandma took my hand and said, "Kathy, let's go check on her."

A little later, Karen and I helped Grandpa rinse off the table. He pulled his handkerchief from his pants pocket, removed his glasses, and dried his lenses. He wiped perspiration from his forehead, then tucked the damp handkerchief into his shirt pocket. He looked tired and snapped, "Let that be a lesson for all of us. Don't poke at someone with hurtful words. Otherwise, you might stir up a hornet's nest, and get your mouth stung." He cracked a smile then asked Karen to toss the rolled newspaper into the burning barrel. He said, "We'll burn garbage after we eat. Don't wanna invite more trouble with varmints or bears!"

I giggled but Karen rolled her eyes. "Grandma told us not to believe anything you say about bears!" Grandpa hunched his shoulders, formed claws with his hands, and growled loudly! We screamed with delight and dashed off to find a new adventure.

Chapter Ten
Reunion with Family

"Though leaves are many, the root is one."
—William Butler Yeats

Cicadas buzzed loudly in the trees, a sure sign summer was coming to an end. The early September sunshine felt hot on my face. Karen and I anxiously sat on the clubhouse steps, watching the road. Karen's glum expression reflected our mixed emotions about Labor Day weekend and our family's anticipated arrival. I wanted to reunite with my parents and siblings, but I was sad. Summer vacation with Grandma and Grandpa was over. I glanced at Grandma in the garden. She tugged on tangled, overgrown tomato vines and swatted at a swarm of gnats that stifled her breathing. She coughed and attempted to speak. "We grew a record number of tomatoes this summer, but the last of 'em dropped to the ground." She cleared her throat. "The rabbits have been nibbling on them. Help me dump 'em into the compost bin."

I responded, "Sure, Grandma," but Karen elbowed me and squealed. On the gravel road, a cloud of dust trailed behind our old brown family station wagon. When the car came to a halt, Mom leaned out the passenger side window and cried, "Hi, girls!" Dad waved as he walked to the back of the car. He unlatched the tailgate to release Eddie and Jane who were buckled into the rear seat facing backwards. My younger sister Jane rushed into the garden to hug Grandma.

Mom gently woke Joe from his nap and unbuckled his seat belt. I cuddled my sweet baby sister, Rosie, in my arms. Eddie ran toward the dock, cupped his hands around his mouth, and shouted, "Hello, Mississippi!" His voice reverberated through the channel. At the top of the clubhouse stairs, Grandpa warned, "Eddie, stay off the dock until I come down!"

Everyone pitched in and carried what they could up to the porch. After the car trunk was unpacked, Grandpa set up the grill. I stood next to Dad who filled an old coffee can with charcoal cubes. When he squirted them with lighter fluid, a faint smell like mineral spirits tickled my nose. Dad checked the time on his watch and gestured to stand back. He struck a match and dropped it into the can. Flames leapt out like a dragon's tongue, then receded back inside the can. When the coals turned red, Dad knocked the can on its side and used a stick to make a small pile of coals. As they turned white hot, he spread them out and told us to get the meat from the kitchen. Karen and I carefully navigated down the clubhouse steps carrying Tupperware containers, one filled with marinated chicken pieces and the other pork steaks.

Uncle Frank strolled across the lawn. From the porch next door, Aunt Mandy fussed, "Frank, take these desserts to Jane."

He ignored her and picked up his pace. He gritted his pipe between his teeth and grinned. He reached into his baggy overalls' pocket and removed three cans of cold Falstaff beer, one for each of the men. In the kitchen window, Grandpa adjusted the rabbit ears on his radio. He tuned it to his favorite sports channel, and the voices of Jack Buck and Harry Carey spouted their opinions about league teams and players. Grandpa rushed down the stairs and grumbled, "I'm worried about the New York Yankees. Roger Maris and Mickey Mantle are in a heated race to beat Babe Ruth's record."

Uncle Frank piped up, "Yep. Heard Maris got booed during the last game. Everybody loves Mickey Mantle."

Dad lowered the grill grates and used a fork to evenly space the meat pieces. They hissed as he basted them with his secret recipe sauce. He joined in, "Well, the Cards have 'Stan the Man' Musial, and he dominates the game. Not to mention he's a great role model on and off the field."

A cry broke the conversation when Aunt Mandy shouted, "Frank!" and waddled across the lawn with two pies. When she handed one to Uncle Frank, she smiled and asked him nicely to follow her up the stairs.

The radio crackled, lost reception, and Grandpa squawked, "Jane, when we get back to town, remind me to buy a new radio!"

Grandma unplugged the radio and announced through the window, "We're ready! Time for supper!"

Mom gathered up the kids, except Eddie. He had to be called a few times. Grandpa grinned knowingly and pointed to the tent. Eddie was playing with a frog.

Dad shouted, "Time to eat! Come wash your hands!"

Karen led the way up the stairs while I guided Jane and Joey by holding their hands. The kitchen table was covered by a red checked cloth. Place settings were laid out for each family member. In the center was a bowl of coleslaw, potato salad, freshly baked bread, and a small dish of churned butter. Grandpa used two thick phone books to create a booster seat for Joe. Grandma brought in an old wooden highchair for Rosie and tucked rolled towels around her. Dad placed platters of pork steaks and marinated chicken at the head of the table. He closed his eyes and placed his right hand above his eyebrow. That was his signal to pray.

"Bless us, oh Lord, and these thy gifts which we are about to receive from thy bounty, through Christ our Lord. Amen."

Eddie sounded off, "God is good. God is great. Let's EAT!"

Dad furrowed his brows and in his deep voice said, "In this family, we say our prayers in a respectable way."

Eddie grinned, grabbed a chicken leg, and took a big bite. I started to giggle but bit my tongue.

Aunt Mandy reminded us, "Leave room for pie. One is blueberry, and one is peach."

After the pies were devoured, Mom put Rosie down to sleep. Aunt Mandy stood next to Grandma at the sink and chatted about grocery specials at the Elsberry General Store. Jane wanted to help, so we handed her a plastic dish to dry while we put the rest away.

Grandpa and Dad meandered down to the boat with the boys and took them for a short ride. I overheard Grandpa say, "The river is calm, and the fresh air will make them sleep like babies." After they returned, Grandpa and Dad built a small fire inside a circle of stacked stones. They reclined in folding chairs and stretched their legs. Grandpa smoked a few cigarettes while Dad whittled a tree branch and poked the embers with it. Above, shades of violet and indigo unfurled across the sky. After sunset, the outline of the slim crescent moon shimmered on the murky river's surface. My brothers settled into their sleeping bags while Jane, Karen, and I nestled into our cots on the porch. The river softly sloshed against its banks, and I closed my eyes. I whispered my favorite prayer that

Grandma taught me: "Now I lay me down to sleep. I pray the Lord my soul to keep. May angels watch me through the night and wake me with the morning light."

Chapter Eleven
Cats Playin' Fiddles

Normandy, Missouri

June 1970

*"Perhaps they are not stars in the sky
but rather openings where our loved ones shine down
to let us know they are happy."*
—Eskimo saying

Karen and I continued to have occasional sleepovers at Grandma and Grandpa's house for the next ten years, and we happily spent summer vacations at the clubhouse. But things changed the year I entered high school. Karen got her driver's license and took a part-time job at Quillman's Drugstore in downtown Ferguson. I started babysitting for my family and the neighbors. I missed visits with Grandma and Grandpa, but it seemed there was never enough time.

One day, Karen dropped me off at their house, and I climbed the steps two at a time. Grandma slowly opened the door. Although her bright eyes appeared tired, she greeted me with a tight hug.

Grandpa sat at the kitchen table, sipping a cold cup of coffee. He cleared his throat and said, "Let's fill up the bird feeders. They've been empty for a while."

I followed him outside, and as I scooped up the seed from the can, I noticed his faraway gaze. He grimaced and groaned as he grasped the rusty rail up to the house. I took his free hand and helped him through the door.

Grandma spread out a fresh linen tablecloth and said, "Kathy, we're having your favorite, chicken and dumplings. Stay for supper."

Grandpa glanced at the cat clock and said, "Looks like Mandy and Frank are late again."

I realized Grandpa thought they were still alive. Grandma looked directly into my eyes and gently patted his hand. In that instant, I knew. Grandpa's memory was no longer sharp as a tack.

On a sweltering summer night in June, the phone rang after everyone had gone to bed. I sat straight up then tiptoed down the hall. I overheard Mom say, "What is it? What's wrong?"

I faintly heard my grandmother's voice. Then Mom said, "We'll leave right away."

Karen snuck up beside me and asked, "What's going on?"

I shrugged. I was concerned and said, "Sounds like we're going to Grandma and Grandpa's house."

Karen whispered, "Now? In the middle of the night?"

We all fumbled around to get dressed. Before we walked out the door, Dad told Karen to drive the old station wagon and handed her the keys. He said, "Mom and I will drive ahead and bring the kids in the new car. Don't drive too fast. OK?"

The car doors squeaked when Karen and I got in. The red light on the dashboard blinked 2:34 a.m. Karen tuned the radio to her favorite station. A Beatles song played, and I softly hummed along. Karen carefully parked on the street in front of the house. The new car was parked in the driveway. I thought the porch light seemed dim. As usual, Karen led the way up the steps. As I lingered behind, an image of my Barbie suitcase popped into my mind. I stopped for a moment, and a feeling of dread weighed heavily on my heart. When the front door opened, Grandma was shrouded by a light behind her. She didn't reach out for a hug. In a trembling voice, she said, "Grandpa's resting in the bedroom. Why don't you go see him? I'll be in the kitchen with your mom and dad. We put the younger kids to bed."

I nodded. My vision clouded with tears and my heart ached.

When I entered the room, Grandpa was asleep in his four-poster bed. His face was thin and pasty white. He startled us when he coughed and attempted to clear his throat. He pointed his shaky finger to the ceiling corner and mumbled, "See them cats?" He squinted and grumbled louder. "Them cats! Hear 'em? They're playin' fiddles on the steamboat!" He winced before he cried, "Pops, I brought the secret bait, and I can hear the fish drumming below the boat."

Grandpa's breathing turned shallow and seemed labored. I sniffled and tears streamed down my face. Grandma came into the bedroom and sat on the edge of the bed. She smoothed the quilt around Grandpa's chest, leaned toward his ear, and whispered, "Roy, the family is here. Pops is waiting for you."

I held my breath and felt heat rise in my cheeks. I trembled and swiped at flowing tears. I choked, "Grandma, I'm scared," and Karen started to cry. Grandma led us into the living room, and we sat down on her little gray couch. My mind whirred with memories. I grabbed some Kleenex tissues from a box on the side table and stared at the marbles in the fishbowl. I tried to compose myself, but I was overwhelmed with sadness and sobbed uncontrollably.

Karen pointed at our piggy banks on the shelf and murmured, "Look, Kath. Grandpa repaired my bank with glue just like he promised."

Grandma inhaled deeply and spoke in a soothing way. "Now there… I understand how you feel. We had great fun with Grandpa, didn't we?" She paused to gather her thoughts. "He loved spending time with you, playing pirates, watering the flowers, chasing after you in the yard as you skipped around twirling your umbrellas. Remember? Grandpa taught you how to fish, and those adventures meant the world to him. He told me he was blessed to see you grow up into the beautiful young ladies you've become."

Grandma glanced out the picture window and gazed upon the waning crescent moon surrounded by twinkling stars. "Grandpa is ready to leave the life he had here on earth and the people who loved him. Always remember how much he loved us. He will wait for me in Heaven, and when I get there, we'll wait together for you." Grandma pulled the girls in close, placed her hand over her heart, and whispered, "That's a promise."

In loving memory...

Louis Leroy "Roy" Bode
Born 8-23-1897
Died 6-30-1970
Mt. Lebanon Cemetery
St. Louis County, Missouri

Epilogue

After Grandpa died, Grandma moved into a nearby apartment. She loved her home but keeping up with Grandpa's gardens and bird feeders was too much, and I worried about the steps to the laundry area. The apartment was small, so she kept only her most cherished possessions and memories. The little gray couch was a good fit for the small living room. Grandma asked Dad to hang the picture of the woman playing a piano above it. The fishbowl and marbles rested on the side table. The pair of goldfish had long ago died, but the plant flourished.

As Karen and I unpacked her kitchen dishes, Grandma put on her apron, stirred up a pot of chicken and dumplings, and patiently listened as Karen and I chatted about college life and boys. I told Grandma how much I appreciated her letters and the five-dollar bills she tucked inside to brighten my days. When I came home on breaks, I talked with her for hours. She had a way of listening to me and making me feel loved. After I got engaged my junior year, I asked Grandma to sew my dress. I was thrilled when she added special touches like tiny pearl buttons on the sleeves. It reminded me of Grandma's wedding gown in the attic, and how beautiful it was. When my son Tim was born, Grandma started a tradition and quilted a unique baby blanket for each of my children. Her hands were riddled with arthritis, but she paid great attention to the stitches, and we all treasured them.

Grandma remained healthy until the last year of her life. When she started having chest pains, the cardiologist told her triple bypass surgery would extend her life, but he had never done it on someone her age. The procedure was performed two days before her ninety-fifth birthday. My sister Karen, a cardiac nurse, assured her that she was in good hands. The surgery went well, and she was able to stay at Mom's house to recuperate. Grandma was weak but comfortable in the guest room. Mom placed an old cow bell next to her bed to ring when Grandma needed assistance. I still have it.

On a lovely spring day in April, Mom called with the news that Grandma had passed away. I was overwhelmed with sadness. I loved her dearly, and she was my best friend. I wondered in silence as tears streamed down my face if Grandma had died in her sleep. Was it a peaceful transition? I wish I had been there.

Mom told me about the extraordinary moments before she died and said Grandma reached both arms high in the air and smiled. I shivered and imagined Grandpa welcoming her into his arms. Later that day, I heard a pair of cardinals singing and spotted them in my cherry blossom tree. It was a beautiful sight, and as they sang, my heart was filled with peace.

In loving memory ...

Jane Rebecca Licklider

Born 1-13-1895

Died 4-18-1990

Mt. Lebanon Cemetery

St. Louis County, Missouri

Author's Note

Finding Our Fate on Fayette
Springfield, Illinois
2000

I leisurely strolled with my husband George down the walking path in Washington Park. In late January, mother nature had granted us a reprieve, a hopeful reminder that spring would eventually arrive. The warm sun was golden against the blue sky. Glittering pine trees dripped with melting snow. The park was abuzz with activity. Familiar holiday songs chimed from the Thomas Rees Memorial Carillon bells. Children played on slides and swings while their mothers visited. We walked out of the park onto Fayette Street, enchanted by the charming neighborhood.

A bright red cardinal dipped up and down into the trees ahead. It perched on a "For Sale by Owner" sign, then disappeared when his female partner called. The gray house, trimmed in faded red and green, was dwarfed by a huge oak tree. A thin layer of moss covered the roof. A light breeze gently rocked the wood porch swing, and I felt compelled to approach.

I turned to George and said encouragingly, "Let's be brave and introduce ourselves to the owners." He reluctantly followed me up the steps. As I raised my hand to knock, the door opened. A woman with silver hair and slate blue eyes greeted me with a smile. She wore a flowered blue apron and her resemblance to Grandma was unnerving. I said, "We saw the sign and we'd like to arrange a tour."

She sweetly replied, "My daughter is the owner. If you give me your name and number, I'll let her know you're interested. You can look around while I find a paper and pen."

I stepped inside and immediately felt at home. A pleasant aroma drifted from the kitchen. Two little girls raced around the corner shaking paper bags. I had a flashback to memories with Grandma and asked, "Are those homemade fried donuts?" The younger girl smiled and offered me one.

I peeked into the living room. It was spacious and filled with natural light. George liked the heart-of-pine wood flooring. Two carved pillars and swirled marble tiles framed the fireplace. An antique brass screen like the one in Abraham Lincoln's home protected the logs that burned with small flames. Sunlight from the seeded bay windows directed my attention to a portrait above the mantel. I walked closer. I stared at it. A woman in a red velvet dress played a grand piano. I felt a chill.

I recalled a childhood memory of exploring Grandma's attic. I wondered aloud, "George, what happened to Grandma's picture like this one? It was in her apartment before she passed away." He shrugged, and I thought, "I must find its whereabouts."

As we descended the steps, a pair of cardinals perched on the swing sang to us. I turned to George and remarked, "I love this house. It's charming and close to the park. The only thing missing is a fishpond with a bench where I can reminisce and share memories with our grandchildren." I looked up at the clear blue sky and said a prayer of hope and gratitude to Grandma for leading the way.

Photographs

The larger group was tak-
in 1912 and it is the same
ilding with the porch added,
e Teacher was J.S. Fitz-
patrick, the flag bearers were
Willie Branson and MaryCal-
vin. The little boy holding
the identification slate was
Wayne Branson. Others n
be recognized but we cl
the story and pass on leav
you the memories,

The larger group was taken in 1912 and it is the same building with the porch added. The Teacher was J.S. Fitzpatrick, the flag bearers were Willie Branson and Mary Calvin. The little boy holding the identification slate was Wayne Branson. Others may be recognized but we close the story and pass on leaving you the memories.

The pupils in the picture were attending a summer school in 1896 and Miss Mamie Johnson was the teacher. They are Elsie Matlock, Louise Jacobs, Viola Licklider, Mabel Short, Clara Licklider, Annie Licklider, Mabel Sewell, Lizzie Heironimous, John Anderson, Joe Keruper, Walter Sorrell, Arthur Short and Arvel Branson.

The pupils in the picture were attending a summer school in 1896 and Miss Mamie Johnson was the teacher. They are Elsie Matlock, Louise Jacobs, Viola Licklider, Mable Short, Clara Licklider, Annie Licklider, Mabel Sewell, Lizzie Heironimous, John Anderson, Joe Keruper, Walter Sorrrell, Arthur Short and Arvel Branson.

John Louis Bode, grandfather of Roy

15-year-old, Jane Rebecca Licklider,
ready to board train to St. Louis

Grandma Jane, Normandy, MO 1960
-waiting for her girls

Jane's mother, Alice, with her turkeys

*Jane's mother, Alice,
wearing her black straw hat*

*Ernest Wycoff, fiance of Jane Licklider.
Killed in World War 1.*

Karen and Kathy with their umbrellas
on Grandma's back porch in June, 1960.

Stilt house on Mississippi River, Elsberry, MO.
Frank and Mandy's house in the background

Grandpa Roy and Grandma Jane
with their catch of the day.

109

Joey and Eddie holding their fish, August, 1968

Kathy and Karen on log at the
Mississippi River Sandbar.

Kathy's dad, Ed, grilling. Toddler, Joey, with fishing pole.

House on Fayette; Springfield, IL, 2001.

Marvelous Family Recipes

from

Marbles in a Fishbowl

Pinwheel Cookies

Ingredients

3 cups flour
1 teaspoon baking powder
1 teaspoon salt
1 ½ cups granulated sugar
1 cup butter
2 large eggs (room temperature)
1 teaspoon vanilla extract
¼ cup cocoa powder

Steps

1. In a bowl, whisk flour, baking powder, and salt.
2. In a separate bowl, beat sugar and butter.
3. Add eggs and vanilla. Stir until combined.
4. Gradually beat dry ingredients into the mixture.
5. Remove half of the dough and set aside.
6. Add and mix cocoa powder into the remaining dough.
7. On parchment paper, roll plain dough into a 9-inch x 14-inch rectangle.

8. In the same manner, roll chocolate dough on a piece of parchment paper.

9. Lift the parchment with the chocolate dough, and carefully flip it upside down onto the plain dough.

10. Leave the top paper on and gently roll doughs together to ¼-inch thickness.

11. Peel away the top piece of paper and discard.

12. Starting on the 14-inch side, roll dough into a tight roll.

13. Wrap in the parchment. Chill one hour or longer.

14. Preheat oven to 350 degrees.

15. Line a baking sheet with parchment paper.

16. Unwrap dough. Using a sharp knife, slice into ½-inch pieces. Place on baking sheet about 1 inch apart.

17. Bake 8 - 10 minutes. (They will look pale.)

18. Remove cookies and cool on a wire rack.

Enjoy!

Fried Donuts

Coatings

½ cup granulated sugar and ¾ teaspoon of ground cinnamon

½ cup of powdered sugar

Ingredients

1 can Pillsbury Grands! Flaky Layers Original Biscuits

(8 count/16.3 ounces. Red Label.)

2 cups vegetable oil

Instructions

1. Separate dough into eight biscuits, then place on parchment paper.
2. Use a 1-inch plastic cap or cookie cutter to punch a hole in each biscuit. Push out the centers.
3. In a 2-quart heavy saucepan, heat oil to 350 degrees, using a digital thermometer.

4. Otherwise, dip a wood spoon or chopstick into the oil. When small bubbles form, the oil is ready.

5. Carefully place two to three biscuits into the oil. Fry on one side until golden.

6. Use prongs or a large slotted spoon to carefully turn and fry the other side.

7. Remove and place onto a cooling rack or plate.

8. Carefully place four to eight donut holes into oil. Gently roll them to fry the other side until golden.

9. Remove and place on a wire rack or plate. Cool about three minutes.

10. While donuts are warm, place into a paper bag containing coating and gently shake.

11. Otherwise, turn warm donuts and holes in a bowl until coated.

Enjoy!

Buttermilk Pancakes

Ingredients (Makes 8 - 10)

1 cup flour
2 ¼ teaspoons baking powder
2 teaspoons granulated sugar
½ teaspoon salt
2 small/medium eggs or 1 large/extra-large egg
1 cup of buttermilk
2 tablespoons butter, melted

Steps

1. In a small bowl, sift or whisk flour, baking powder, sugar, and salt.
2. Separate egg yolks from the whites. Set whites aside.
3. In a medium bowl, combine yolks, buttermilk, and melted butter.
4. Use a wood spoon to sprinkle and blend in dry ingredients to form batter. Do not overmix.
5. Whisk the whites until stiff peaks form and hold. Gently fold whites into batter.

6. Allow the batter to rest for 10 minutes. Do not stir again.

7. Place an ungreased griddle pan on medium-high heat. Wait about two minutes.

8. Drop water from your fingertip into the pan. When it sizzles, the pan is ready.

9. Fill a ¼ measuring cup with batter or use a ladle to form 4-inch pancakes.

10. Bubbles will rise and pop. When they pop in the center, carefully slide a spatula underneath and flip.

11. When the centers stop rising, gently press down about 3 seconds. Uncooked batter will spread and cook.

12. Turn off the heat, and place pancakes on plates. Serve with fresh butter, maple syrup, or elderberry jelly.

Enjoy!

Maple Syrup

Ingredients

1 cup water

1 cup brown sugar (packed)

1 cup granulated sugar

1 tablespoon maple flavor extract

Steps

1. In a saucepan, bring water and sugars to a boil over medium-high heat.
2. Stir constantly. Reduce heat to medium-low. Add maple extract.
3. Reduce heat to a simmer and continue to stir about two more minutes.
4. Remove pan from heat.
5. Carefully pour warm syrup into a small ceramic pitcher for use.

Enjoy!

- Store leftover syrup in an airtight container and refrigerate up to three months.

Homemade Butter

Ingredients

1 cup heavy whipping cream

¼ teaspoon salt (optional)

Steps

1. Pour heavy whipping cream into a plastic jar.
2. Tighten the lid and then shake vigorously for three to four minutes.
3. Stop shaking it when you hear a sloshing sound.
4. Drain the liquid.
5. Add 1 cup of cold water. Shake one minute.
6. Drain again.
7. Repeat steps five and six until liquid appears almost clear (1-2 more times).
8. Optional: For salted butter, add salt and shake 5 to 10 seconds.

9. Drop or scoop butter onto a piece of parchment paper.

10. Wrap the butter in the paper and leave an opening at the bottom.

11. Squeeze out any remaining liquid.

12. Open the paper and scrape the butter into a clump or ball.

13. Place it in a butter dish. Cover and refrigerate until ready to use.

Enjoy!

- Unsalted butter can be left uncovered at room temperature up to two hours.

- Salted butter can be left uncovered at room temperature up to four hours.

- Refrigerate butter in a covered dish. It will stay fresh up to five days.

Elderberry Jelly

Equipment needed

6 (8-ounce) canning jars

6 new rings and lids

Cheesecloth

Large stock pot and steaming rack

Ingredients

4 pounds ripe elderberries (about 8-10 cups.)

¼ cup lemon juice

4 ½ cups granulated sugar

¼ teaspoon butter

1 Sure Jell pectin (1.75 oz.)

Steps

1. Rinse berries. Remove stems. Simmer berries in a pot and slightly mash.
2. Increase heat to medium. Continue to crush until they reach boiling point.
3. Reduce heat and simmer 10 minutes.
4. Use four layers of cheesecloth or a sieve to strain the berry juice into a large bowl.

Prepare jars

1. Place rack on bottom of a tall, large pot.
2. Add jars and fill pot with water (1 to 2 inches). Cover.
3. Boil for 10 minutes to sterilize.

Next steps

1. Measure 3 cups of strained juice for one batch of jelly, if using Sure Jell pectin.
2. Add lemon juice, berry juice, and pectin. Boil on high.
3. Add sugar and butter. Boil again. Stir with a wood spoon.
4. Do not allow it to boil over. Reduce heat if necessary.
5. Full boil for one minute, then remove from heat.
6. Carefully pour into jars. Fill up to ¼-inch from rim.
7. Use a damp paper towel to wipe rim and remove any drips.
8. Use a sterilized plastic utensil to scrape jar sides and release air. (Bubbles will rise to the top.)

9. Secure the rings, then lids on jars. Do not over tighten. (Any trapped air needs to be released.)

10. Place jars at least 1-inch apart in a water bath for five minutes. (Jars should not touch.)

11. As they cool, the lids should pop when they seal.

Enjoy!

- Store open jars in the refrigerator up to two months.

Chicken Marinade

Special Note:

*The original recipe was made with Falstaff beer, which is no longer in production. Substitute with your preferred lager beer.

Seasoning Ingredients

¾ teaspoon ground sage
¼ teaspoon onion
¼ teaspoon thyme
¼ teaspoon pepper
pinch of ground cloves

Optional- Substitute with 1¾ teaspoon poultry seasoning

Marinade Ingredients

1 small yellow onion
1 tablespoon brown sugar
1 tablespoon granulated sugar
1 teaspoon celery salt
1 cup lager beer
1 cup lager beer
Properly prepared, uncooked chicken, whole or pieces

Instructions

1. Peel yellow onion. On a cutting board, finely chop.
2. Place pieces in a medium/large bowl.
3. Whisk together brown sugar, granulated sugar, and seasoning.
4. Add lager and vigorously whisk for two to three minutes.
5. Measure ½ cup of marinade and set aside.
6. Place chicken pieces into a dish.
7. Pour marinade over them. Cover and refrigerate for one hour.
8. As you grill, baste occasionally using the fresh marinade.

Enjoy!

- **Reminder: It is unsafe to baste with sauce that raw meat has marinated in!**

Pork Steak Marinade

Ingredients

8-ounces Maull's Genuine Classic BBQ Sauce

1 small yellow onion

1 tablespoon brown sugar

1 tablespoon granulated sugar

1 teaspoon celery salt

1 teaspoon garlic powder

Steps

1. Peel yellow onion. On a cutting board, finely chop.
2. Place pieces in a medium/large mixing bowl.
3. Add BBQ sauce and stir.
4. Add brown sugar and granulated sugar. Vigorously whisk.
5. Add celery salt and garlic powder. Whisk until well blended.
6. Measure ½ cup of marinade and set aside.
7. Place steaks in a dish and pour half of the marinade over them.

8. Cover and refrigerate 30 minutes.

9. Remove dish, turn steaks, and pour remaining marinade over them.

10. Cover and refrigerate another 30 minutes.

11. Grill pork steaks until internal temperature reaches 145 degrees.

12. Baste occasionally using the fresh marinade.

Enjoy!

- Reminder: It is unsafe to baste with sauce that raw meat has been marinated in!

Peach Pie

Important Note #1

Prepare fresh peaches. Rinse, then pat dry with a paper towel. Peel with a paring knife. Slice into pieces or chunks. Place into a bowl, cover with lid or plastic wrap, and refrigerate.

Crust Bottom Ingredients

½ cup (8 tablespoons) COLD, unsalted butter

1 ¼ cups all-purpose flour

¼ teaspoon salt

2 tablespoons chilled water

Egg wash: 1 large egg, white only, and 1 tablespoon water blended

- These portions make enough dough to form a 12-inch disk for a 9-inch pie dish.

MARBLES IN A FISHBOWL

Steps

1. Whisk flour and salt in a bowl.
2. Using a pastry cutter or two knives, cut in four tablespoons of butter.
3. Mix in 1 tablespoon of cold water; then cut in the remaining butter.
4. Add one more tablespoon of water and form a ball. Do not overmix.
5. Sprinkle flour on the counter. Use palm to flatten dough, and then cover with a big piece of parchment paper. Use a rolling pin and shape dough into a 10-inch disk, ½-inch thick.
6. Turn the dough over and lightly sprinkle with flour. Use a rolling pin to spread it two more inches (to ¼-inch thick). Do not overwork. Allow the disk to roll and stick on the pin; then transfer and press it into the pie dish. Flute dough with your knuckles. (Do not let it hang over the edge.)
7. Brush egg wash in the bottom to seal it. Cover dish with plastic wrap. Chill 30 minutes.

KATHY LAMSARGIS

Important Note #2
Place ¾ cup (12 tablespoons) unsalted butter sticks into freezer for at least 30 minutes. It will be grated to make the crumbly top crust.

Filling Ingredients
5 cups fresh peaches (peeled, sliced, chilled)

1/3 cup granulated sugar

1/3 cup brown sugar (lightly packed)

½ teaspoon ground cinnamon

½ teaspoon allspice

4 tablespoons cornstarch

1 tablespoon lemon juice

Steps
1. Whisk sugars, cinnamon, allspice, and cornstarch together in a mixing bowl.
2. Remove peaches from the refrigerator and sprinkle with the lemon juice.
3. Gently stir before you add them to the dry ingredients. Mix all ingredients.
4. Remove crust from the refrigerator.
5. Scoop the filling into the chilled crust; then set it aside.

132

Important Note #3
Preheat oven to 425 degrees.

Crumbly Top Crust Ingredients
1½ cups all-purpose flour

1/3 cup of granulated sugar

1/3 cup of brown sugar (packed)

¼ teaspoon salt

¾ cup (12 tablespoons) unsalted butter sticks, frozen

Steps
1. Gently mix flour, sugars, and salt together in a bowl.
2. Remove butter from the freezer and grate it.
3. Add grated butter to the dry ingredients to make a crumbly mixture.
4. Using a large spoon, scoop it over the filling and spread evenly.
5. Put pie dish on a baking sheet, cover edges with foil strips, and place on the center rack.

6. Bake at 425 degrees for 15 minutes.

7. Lower the temperature to 350 degrees and bake for 20 minutes.

8. Carefully remove foil and bake 10-15 minutes. Juices will bubble. Crust will turn golden.

9. Cool for at least 30 minutes; longer is better so the filling can firm up.

Enjoy with ice cream or whipped topping!

Additional Notes

- If you use pre-made Pillsbury crust, review the instructions. They can bake faster and burn.
- Using a clear pie dish is recommended to monitor the color of the crust as it bakes.
- Refrigerate pie for up to three days; freeze it up to two months.

Chicken & Dumplings

Seasoning Ingredients

(Makes 3 teaspoons, but only ¼ teaspoon needed.)
1 teaspoon ground dried sage
¾ teaspoon ground dried thyme
¾ teaspoon ground dried rosemary
¼ teaspoon ground black pepper
¼ teaspoon salt
- Or substitute above with ¼ teaspoon Lawry's Poultry Seasoning

Steps

1. Mix/whisk seasoning ingredients in a small dish.

2. Measure 2 ¾ teaspoons and put into a zip-lock bag. Refrigerate.

3. Measure remaining portion, ¼ teaspoon and set aside.

Chicken & Broth Ingredients

2 teaspoons unsalted butter
½ cup chopped yellow onion
3 celery ribs, chopped or thin slices
2 small-medium carrots, chopped
4 cups chicken broth
4 ounces cream cheese, cubed
2 cups shredded, cooked chicken

Steps

1. On a cutting board, chop the onion into small pieces.
2. In a 5-quart Dutch oven, melt butter over low-medium heat.
3. Add onion to butter and cook two to four minutes until tender.
4. Add broth and seasoning. Stir occasionally.
5. Chop celery and add to the mixture.
6. Chop carrots and add to the mixture.
7. Increase heat to medium-high. Add cubed cream cheese.
8. Stir until melted. Increase heat to medium-high.

9. Add the cooked, shredded chicken. Stir until mixture simmers then reduce heat to low.

10. Cover with the lid, then prepare dumplings.

Dumpling Ingredients

1 ½ cups flour
2 teaspoons baking powder
¾ teaspoon salt
3 tablespoons butter
¾ cup milk

Steps

1. Whisk the flour, baking powder, and salt in a bowl.
2. Using two knives, cut in the butter to create coarse crumbs.
3. Slowly add the milk and form a dough ball. Do not overmix.
4. Using a spoon, scoop out small dough clumps and drop into the broth. (Dough will float.)
5. Leave pan uncovered and cook for 10 minutes.
6. Cover pan with lid and cook for 10 more minutes.
7. Remove from heat.

Enjoy!

Discussion Questions

for

Book Clubs, Families, Grandparents, and Students

Prologue - Mississippi River

1. How do you know Roy is knowledgeable about fishing? Provide examples.
2. How did the mood change after Roy announced he had a big bite? What happened?
3. When the alligator slapped its tail and the canoe rocked, what did Pops tell Roy to do?
   a. What might have happened had Roy argued with Pops or done something else?
   b. Do you think Roy made a wise decision?
   c. How did Edgar, Pops, and Roy each react after the alligator swam away?

Prologue - Oak Grove School

4. Why did the students bully Shorty?
   a. Have you ever been bullied?
   b. If so, how did you feel? What did you do about being bullied?
   c. Do you know someone who has been bullied?
   d. In your opinion, what is the best way to help?

5. Think about how Jane treated Shorty.

    a. How did her kindness affect Shorty?

    b. How did Shorty influence Jane before she moved away?

6. Did Jane teach Shorty the skills he needed to compete?

    a. What did she teach him? What did he learn?

    b. Did Jane let Shorty win, or did he win "fair and square"? Explain in your own words.

Chapter One - First Sleepover

1. What did the fishbowl look like? Describe in detail.

    a. What was at the top?
    b. What was inside?

2. What was Grandma's surprise for Karen and Kathy in the kitchen?

    a. Have you ever made cookies?
    b. Did you make them by yourself or with someone?
    c. What was the occasion?
    d. What are your favorite cookies?

3. When Karen broke the egg, how did Grandma react?

    a. Were you surprised by Grandma's reaction? Why or why not?
    b. Have you ever broken something accidentally? What?
    c. How did others react when it happened?

4. How did Kathy show her affection and appreciation for Grandma?

Chapter Two - Treasures in the Attic

1. What did Grandma say or do to show safety was important to her?

2. What treasures did Karen and Kathy discover in the attic?

   a. Make a list.

   b. Which one would you like to know more about? Why?

3. How did you feel when Grandma shared her story about Ernest?

4. When Grandma said her friends told her, "God must have other plans for you," why do you think they said that?

   a. Have you ever been extremely sad or disappointed?

   b. What happened? What did you think and feel at that time?

   c. How did your family and friends try to comfort or reassure you?

Chapter Three - Bubble Bath and Baby Powder

1. How did Grandma make sleepovers fun? Share examples.

   a. When Grandma said, "I have a treat... no peeking," was the kewpie doll a surprise to you? What made it special?
   b. Share a time when you received a gift from someone.
   c. Share a time when you gave someone a treat.

2. How did Grandpa make sleepovers fun? Share examples.

3. What did you think about Grandma's bedtime story?

   a. How have times changed since your grandparents and parents were young?
   b. What do you have that they didn't? Share some examples.
   c. What kinds of things are you grateful for? Give some examples.

Chapter Four - Pancakes, Petunias, and Unusual Umbrellas

1. How did Grandma make routine meals seem more enjoyable? Explain in detail.

2. When Grandpa tried to teach Karen about watering petunias, what did she do?

   a. How did Grandpa react? Was he angry? What did he do?

   b. When Grandma came outside, what was she holding?

3. Kathy obliged Karen and switched umbrellas.

   a. How did that work out?

   b. What happened?

4. When Kathy stood at the back door, what did she hear Grandma say? Read it aloud.

   a. Do you agree with what Grandma said? Why or why not?

   b. What relationships do you treasure? Why?

Chapter Five - Warsh Day

1. In what season does this chapter take place, and how was it described using the senses of sight, smell, sound, and touch? Provide examples.

2. Descibe the washing machine. How did it work?

3. Describe the clothesline. How was the laundry hung?

4. What happened after Kathy rushed into the house?
    a. When Karen realized the broken bank was hers, how did she react?
    b. What did Grandpa offer to do?

5. What words of wisdom did Grandma say? Be specific.
    c. Have you ever hurt someone's feelings?
    d. Did you ask for forgiveness or hold a grudge?
    e. Are grudges good or bad? Why?

Chapter Six - Trip to the Stilt House

1. What did Grandpa and Grandma do to prepare for the trip? Provide examples.

2. While driving, how did Grandpa make the trip interesting? What did he do or say?

3. Grandpa stopped for gas on their way to the stilt house.

   a. What was different in 1960 compared to getting gas in 2024? Provide examples.
   b. What is still the same? Explain.

4. What did Kathy see and hear when they arrived at the stilt house?

   a. Images?
   b. Sounds?
   c. Smells?

5. How was bathing and sleeping at Grandma's house different from taking a bath and sleeping at the stilt house?

    a. List similarities.

    b. Which way would you prefer? Why?

6. Read aloud the last paragraph.

    a. What images stand out? What sounds?

    b. What do you think might sound like marbles clicking against each other?

Chapter Seven - Fishing on the Mississippi

1. What did Grandma insist Karen and Kathy wear before they got into the boat?

    a. What was her reason?

    b. Do you agree that safety is important when boating or fishing? Why or why not?

2. What did we learn about Grandpa?

    a. Where did he grow up?

    b. What did he do to earn a living?

    c. What were his interests and hobbies?

    d. What other descriptions are mentioned?

3. How did Grandpa react to Karen hastily casting her fishing pole?

    a. What were his casting instructions to Kathy? List them as steps.

    b. Do you think you could follow them? Why or why not?

4. What stood out about Grandpa's first fishing trip with Pops? Make a list.

    a. What did he remember from so long ago?

    b. What did he hear below the boat?

    c. What did he see in the sky?

    d. What caused the flashing lights? What did he see and hear?

    e. What unusual bait did Pops use to catch drum fish?

Chapter Eight - Baby Cora

1. Describe the scene outside as the storm approached.
   a. What happened inside?
   b. What preparations did they take?

2. What scared Karen when she moved her flashlight around the room?

3. The storm jarred Grandma's memory about her sister, Cora.
   a. What season was it in her story? Describe the weather.
   b. What pandemic was spreading across the nation that made Cora sick?

4. What did Grandma do to try to comfort Cora?

5. What was Grandma's dream about?
   a. Describe the details.
   b. What do you think it meant? How did it make you feel?

Chapter Nine - Circle of Stings

1. Grandpa taught Karen and Kathy how to clean fish.

    a. How did you feel about the process?
    b. Do you think you could do it? Why or why not?

2. What was the hidden treasure called? Describe.

3. Who was Aunt Mandy shouting to?

    a. What was she yelling about?
    b. What words did she use to express her anger?
    c. How did you feel about her words and shouting?

4. When Karen and Kathy ran onto the dock, what did they see? Describe the scene.

5. How did Grandpa react after he and Uncle Frank arrived?

    a. What did he do to protect everyone else from being stung?
    b. Did the others respect his instructions? Would you have? Why or why not?

6. Grandpa said, "Let that be a lesson for all of us." What did he mean? Explain in your own words.

Chapter Ten - Reunion with Family

1. Describe Kathy's mixed emotions about her last weekend at the clubhouse.

2. Who was Grandpa listening to on the radio?
    a. What were they talking about?
    b. Who were the baseball players?
    c. What is your favorite sport?
    d. What is your favorite team? Who is your favorite player? Why?

3. Describe the scene in the kitchen.
    a. Does your family eat meals together? Why or why not?
    b. What was Dad's unspoken signal to pray?

4. In the last paragraph, what were the images and sounds in the sky and in the river? Be specific.

Chapter Eleven - Cats Playin' Fiddles

1. After Kathy and Grandpa filled the bird feeders, what did Grandpa do and say that showed his body and mind were declining?

2. When Karen and Kathy made their way up the steps, what image popped up into Kathy's mind? What was she feeling?

3. Describe Grandpa after Kathy entered the bedroom.
    a. How did he look?
    b. What did he do and say that was startling?

4. Why did Grandma take Karen and Kathy into the living room?
    a. Describe their feelings.
    b. What object did Kathy stare at?
    c. What did Karen comment about on the shelf?

5. In what ways did Grandma try to comfort them?
    a. Read aloud the last two paragraphs.
    b. What promise did Grandma make?
    c. What do you think about it?

6. Have you experienced the loss of a loved one?

    a. Who comforted you and how?

    b. If you weren't comforted, what might have helped? Explain.

7. Have you known someone who lost a loved one? Reflect on this.

    a. What were the circumstances? Did you comfort them?

    b. If you had to comfort someone again, would you do anything differently? Why or why not?

About the Author

Over her twenty-year career in the public school system, Kathy Lamsargis taught different grade levels. Kathy achieved a master's degree in reading and currently provides title services for students at St. Patrick Catholic Elementary School.

Kathy has always been enthusiastic about reading. Long ago she recognized how important it is for children to have deep and lasting relationships, especially with their grandparents. Marbles in a Fishbowl is a tribute to her grandparents, Roy and Jane Bode.

She is thrilled to share a slice of their history and the life lessons she learned while spending time with them.

Kathy is a dedicated volunteer at St. Martin de Porres Center and also assists other nonprofit organizations with projects throughout the year. After she joined International AssistMedical Missions (IAMM), she traveled to Haiti and Nicaragua six times to help disadvantaged multi-generational families.

Kathy and her husband George reside in Springfield, Illinois, where she has lived since 1980 after relocating from Ferguson, Missouri, where she grew up. They have a blended family of four grown children: Tim, Carrie, Betsy, and Sophie. They also have twelve grandchildren: Atticus, Archer, Ricky, Anna, Kate, Tommy, Layne, Demi, Paige, Halle, Isaac, and Anderson.

Contact Information

Thank you for purchasing *Marbles in a Fishbowl*. We hope you enjoyed the book and will let others know about it who would also like to read it.

You may contact the author at *kathylamsargisauthor@gmail.com*.

To order multiple copies through the author, contact her through her website *kathylamsargis.net*.

Printed in the USA
CPSIA information can be obtained
at www.ICGtesting.com
LVHW011609271024
794901LV00003B/582